# THE BIG
# PICTURE

HARPER WAVE

www.harperwave.com

# THE BIG PICTURE

## 11 LAWS THAT WILL CHANGE YOUR LIFE

# TONY HORTON

WITH DENIS FAYE

This book is written as a source of information only. The information contained in this book should by no means be considered a substitute for the advice of a qualified medical professional, who should always be consulted before beginning any new diet, exercise, or other health program.

FIRST EDITION

*Designed by William Ruoto*

---

Library of Congress Cataloging-in-Publication Data

Horton, Tony (Anthony Sawyer).
The big picture : 11 laws that will change your life / Tony Horton.—First edition.
        pages   cm
ISBN 978-0-06-228239-2
1. Change (Psychology). 2. Self-actualization (Psychology). I. Title.
BF637.C4H674   2014
158.1—dc23                                                    2013039249

---

14  15  16  17  18   OV/RRD   10 9 8 7 6 5 4 3 2 1

*This book is dedicated to the love of my life: my sweet, smart, and beautiful Shawna. I feel blessed every day that I'm the guy who gets to call her my best friend and love.*

# CONTENTS

# INTRODUCTION

**W**ill this book change your life?

The information within these pages changed mine. My hope is that you'll gain some benefit from this hard-won knowledge, too. Give me a few hours of your time and I'll tell you everything I know to help you become stronger, healthier, happier, and better in every way. And we're not just going to look at how to change your body; we're going to look at how to shift your attitude, excel at the things you love (and even the things you don't), and improve your relationships with friends, family, and the world at large. We're going to look at how you can make your life better by connecting all of these dots and looking at the Big Picture.

Some people are reluctant to take a step back and really look at their lives. I get it. I've been there (stay tuned for more on that). After all, it's not easy to admit weakness or failure, and it's even less easy to change. But if you're not willing to turn a critical eye on yourself, if you're not someone who sees the value in change, well, you might as well put this book down now. I couldn't help you change a twenty if your fingers were made out of five-dollar bills.

How do you know if you're one of these "stuck" people? Let me ask you: Why did you buy this book? Were you hoping that I'd give you my secret recipe for six-pack abs? Want to know how to drop fifteen pounds in two weeks before your high school reunion? Are you looking for bulging biceps? A hot bikini body?

If the answer is "yes" to any of these questions, I'm not your man. There's nothing wrong with wanting to look your best, but what truly motivates and sustains you should go much, much deeper than muscle definition. Focusing on how you hope to look in the future based on what you're doing now, that's just ego. And let me tell you, your ego is nothing but a mean and cruel deceptive little freak living inside your head that will never bring joy and happiness to your life. What that ego will bring is frustration, depression, manipulation, and fear.

It works a lot like that old gem "money can't buy happiness." You buy things that might make you happy for a day or two, but ultimately, you just end up buying more things to maintain that high. Similarly, when you make changes in your life for aesthetic reasons, you're never going to be content.

If you want to change yourself so that you can be healthier, happier, more productive, and more successful—if you want to be the best possible you—then by all means, pull up a chair, put on your thinking cap, and keep reading. You and me, we're going to do something special.

## WHAT'S THIS "BIG PICTURE" THING?

The Big Picture is all about recognizing your role on this spinning blue marble we call home. You can do this in two simple steps. First, find your true self.

I believe that starts with the body. Throughout this book, I'll address the physical, mental, and emotional components of each of my 11 Laws. All three components are on equal footing, but if you want the second two to work, my advice is to start with the first one. You can go to all the motivational seminars and read all the self-help books you want, but if your mechanics aren't right, you're still not going to function properly. You are a machine. (Don't take that personally. We're all machines.) Your brain is connected to the rest of your body not just by your spine, but also by an amazingly complex system of nerves, blood vessels, and hormones. Your muscles, blood, lungs, heart, digestive system—the whole enchilada (speaking of digestive system)—influences the way you think and feel. If your machine isn't highly tuned and well cared for, all of the daily affirmations in the world aren't going to make a difference; you'll just be dancing the one-step-forward, two-steps-back tango (on repeat).

If you want your life to be what you want it to be, your machine will need to function properly. If you have an overweight, inactive machine and you feed it lousy fuel, I don't care how smart you are, you'll never truly find a sense of adventure, curiosity, and productivity that will allow you to discover your authentic self. Solid diet and exercise stimulate a smorgasbord of beneficial chemicals in your brain. Being fit and healthy allows you to do the things you've always wanted to do—to hop on that horse or that Harley or whatever else you feel like hopping on today.

Maybe you're dealing with some physical limitations that don't allow you to get to the level of fitness you'd like to achieve. That's okay; your life can still be just as amazing as the next person's. Just do your best with what you have. Anyone should be able to eat right and take time to relax—and most people can do some form of exercise. Your limitations may be challenges, but they shouldn't be excuses.

That goes for the rest of you, too: no excuses! Think about it. There are so many things in life you can't control, but what you put in your mouth and what you do physically, those are completely up to you. The weather, your kids, family, work, traffic, all those things might throw your mental and emotional state into a tizzy. But the two things you can control—your discipline to exercise and eat right—will allow you to find solutions as opposed to being stuck in the problem. They can provide true answers for your true self. Once you've established that, it's inevitable that you'll start to change the world around you.

I can almost hear you saying, "'Change the world?' Has Horton gone hippie on us?" Don't worry, folks. Yes, I may eat the occasional bowl of nuts and granola, but the path to the Big Picture has nothing to do with transcendental meditation or the Grateful Dead. I'm not asking you to exercise and eat right in hopes of becoming Gandhi Jr., Mother Teresa Jr., or Martin Luther King Jr. Jr. No, you should treat your body well because doing so is crucial to your long-term happiness. And isn't happiness everyone's goal?

And for those of you out there mumbling, "I'm too busy because of kids, work, or (insert excuse here)," just table that notion for now, okay? I know at least two dozen people with five kids and full-time jobs who still manage to stay healthy. They're crazy busy people, but they're also fit, satisfied, happy people. What makes them different from you? It's a question of discipline, purpose, priorities, and a plan—all tools I'm going to give you in this book.

And here's another motivational tidbit to get you off the couch. To give the best possible care to others, you need to take care of yourself first. Buddhist teacher Thich Nhat Hanh offers a widely quoted analogy on this lesson: If you're in an airplane and the oxygen masks come down, you need to put on your mask before you can help anyone else with theirs. You're no good to anyone if you can't breathe! If you want to support, provide for, and care for the people around you, you need to be at your best. Otherwise, you'll just drag them down with you.

## FROM HUGE TO HERO

Take my buddy Richard Neal. He started his journey at 426 pounds—he was so heavy that his electronic scale simply listed his weight as "ERR." (He had to weigh himself on an industrial scale at a local recycling center.) "I had to make a change," he tells me. "I couldn't do it anymore. Either I was going to die or kill myself."

Thankfully, he chose a third option. He picked up a copy of my workout program *Power 90* and got busy. He changed his lifestyle, including his diet. The pounds melted off. One day, he stepped on his scale and instead of an error message, he saw the most beautiful number in the world: 399. Then 398, 397, 396 . . .

And as the pounds melted away, the burden didn't just lift from his frame, it lifted from his mind. As he puts it, "It changed me emotionally and spiritually." With a lot of hard work and a little help from some DVDs, today Richard has dropped more than 240 pounds and 22 pants sizes—but that's just a tiny part of the impact his weight loss has had on his life. In his darkest times, his doctor told him that he wouldn't live past thirty and he'd never be able to have children. Today, at twenty-nine, Richard has every intention of being part of his one-year-old son Brady's life for decades to come. His metaphorical oxygen mask is firmly in place. "I'm so grateful to know that I'll be able to give him a legacy showing him that he can do whatever he wants to do," he says.

Before his transformation, Richard did his best to be his true self. He seemed like a happy-go-lucky guy, but on the inside, he was miserable. He had a great smile, he had a kind of sense of humor, but he was hiding behind all kinds of mental and emotional baggage. He'd force others to set low expectations for him, because he knew that would make it harder for him to fail.

He was living in the shadows, pretending everything was okay. He wasn't a bad person—he was doing the best he could based on what he had—but given that he could barely help himself, he was in no position to help others. He couldn't even see his toes. How was he going to see the Big Picture?

Today, he's the happy, healthy, productive man, striving to make a "positive thumbprint on the world." He's living an authentic life—and doing his best to spread the message of fitness and nutrition to others. He advises his friends and family and hosts Fit Clubs, where he invites the community in his small town to work out with him. He's living a life that's real, that feels good, that brings joy to him and everyone around him.

Those last four words are huge. Let's take a moment to soak them in. "And everyone around him." This is a major part of seeing the Big Picture. It's not about him anymore. It's not about you, or me, or any other individual. It's about us. It's about how we make our own lives better and how, when we do that, we affect each other as a community.

## HOW TO USE THIS BOOK

Human beings are social creatures. We stopped picking nits out of each other's hair a few thousand years ago, but still, we like to hang out. We play and watch team sports, and go to restaurants, church, concerts, and the movies. We find comfort in sharing those experiences with each other.

Because of this, we tend to follow new trends fairly quickly, simply because it makes it easier to remain within the group. We learn from our friends and family what normal is and we build it into our lifestyles. Sometimes, these trends aren't that important—like wearing skinnier jeans or switching from eight-tracks to MP3s. Sometimes, they're great—like the growing awareness of the benefits of organic foods or yoga. But sometimes, they're bad news—like our current lifestyle. Today, two-thirds of America is overweight, with Canada and Europe not far behind. One-third of adults are obese. There's lots of talk about change, with public service announcements and various bans, rules, and restrictions . . . but where's that getting us? We also have larger seats at movie theaters, seat belt extenders in cars and planes, and home bathroom scales that go to four hundred pounds. "Vanity sizing" is now a common practice in the clothing industry. XL is the new medium. Think you're losing weight because those new size-two Gap khakis seem loose? Surprise! They're actually a size six.

Let's face it: We're an unhealthy, unhappy country and we urgently need to fix that. We're on a treadmill going backward. Increased incidence of diabetes, cancer, heart ailments, emotional disorders, and metabolic syndrome are all symptoms of this new normal. Depression and anxiety have become a way of life, with more than one in ten Americans popping antidepressants as if they were Skittles—that's a 400 percent increase since the eighties! We're miserable, gulping down caffeine, alcohol, and prescription pills to lift us up, settle us down, or just maintain sanity. And what's even scarier is that this behavior has been passed down from parents to kids as a habit, making it almost impossible to break.

Luckily, there's another aspect of the human condition that

can come into play here. As a race, we happen to excel in finding ways out of "almost impossible" situations. Wars, plagues, financial crises, disco. We've surmounted all these things. And now we need to turn our focus to our health.

Research shows that both obesity and depression spread like a virus. If you're surrounded by overweight, miserable people, you have a greater chance of becoming overweight and/or miserable yourself. With this in mind, I want you to become the antivirus. Lead the way and improve your health, happiness, and productivity. (How are you going to do that? Well, that's the whole point of this book . . .) I hate to go all John Lennon here, but just imagine all the people—every individual, every family, every company, every town, and every county—turning their lives around. Imagine how that would affect all of us. That's what the Big Picture is. It's about getting your act together, taking accountability for your life, and making better choices, all while keeping in the back of your mind how that affects other people in your life.

I'm sure that some of my more cynical readers are saying, "Easier said than done, Tony." You're right, it's not an easy road, but we can do it. And I want to guide you on this journey.

## 11 LAWS THAT COVER ALL THE BASES

Some of you might be familiar with my original 11 Laws of Fitness, or even my 11 Laws of Nutrition, but what you're about to read goes beyond those. I've taken those 22, added a few new ones, and distilled the brew down to 11 *new* laws intended to cover all aspects of health and wellness. (If I've missed something, shoot me an email and I'll get on it. That's why God invented paperback editions.)

In each chapter, I'll introduce you to a law. Then we'll dig deep into that law. My goal is to help you be the best possible you, physically, mentally, and emotionally, but I'll tell you right now that there's a lot of emphasis on fitness and nutrition in these laws. I am, after all, a fitness guy. If Tony Danza wrote a self-help book, he'd teach you how to figure out who's the boss. Tony Hawk could tell you how to ride the half-pipe of life. Tony the Tiger would show you how corn and high-fructose corn syrup can make you happy (good luck with that one). For me, it all starts with exercise and eating.

The 11 Laws are all connected in some way to health and fitness, but each of them also has larger life applications. I want to show you how these principles have helped guide my life, and how they've helped others change their lives for the better.

I'll also share some practical strategies, as well as interviews with the people who have influenced me: the experts I consult to keep this domino chain going. The people you look to for help are pivotal to making the shift to a better you. The experts I've talked to throughout this book all helped open my eyes and influenced my shift. A solid mentor helps make growth and change a relatively painless process. That's how it should be: natural and easy. A good coach, a good mentor, a good teacher, a good boss, or a good friend makes change easier.

## TAKE YOUR TIME

You don't need to plow through all 11 Laws in one reading. There's a lot of information here. Take your time. Read the ones you need now and really soak them in. Then come back later for the others. My 11 Laws are there for you whenever you need them, like a twenty-four-hour wisdom convenience mart, only without the slushies, gray hot dogs, and pork rinds.

If you're still reading, it means you care enough about yourself to create the best life you can have. It means that you're brave enough to abandon old, comfortable habits and make positive changes. It means that you're smart enough to know that spending a few hours with a book, getting honest and digging deep, is an investment in your future. That getting committed and doing the work are the keys to happiness and prosperity.

It means you're my kind of people. You have a notion of the Big Picture but you just need a few tools to get you on your way. So step into my toolshed, friends. Grab a hammer and let's get busy.

# THE BIG PICTURE

# DO YOUR BEST AND FORGET THE REST

*Satisfaction lies in the effort, not in the attainment; full effort is full victory.*
—MAHATMA GANDHI

My life is filled with challenges—and I like it that way. For example, as I write this book, I'm also in the middle of developing a new workout program, one of my most ambitious yet. I want it to push the boundaries of fitness . . . and that requires me to push my own boundaries, too.

When I was preparing for the Pilates workout, I was nervous. I mean, I'm familiar with the practice and I've been doing it on my own for a while, but this was my first time demonstrating the moves on camera. So I did the same thing I do every time I'm faced with something challenging: I put in the legwork (literally, in some cases). I studied. I read. I watched. I trained. I surrounded myself with people who could help me learn. And when the day of the shoot arrived, I stepped onto that soundstage like I owned it, knowing I had done the best I could to prepare and would do the best I could to knock it out of the park.

But it's taken effort to get to this point. I've done my homework when it comes to confronting my fears and anxieties. Thanks to that, I have the tools to get the job done. I wasn't feeling nearly as composed leading up to my first on-camera trainer gig back in 1996—as a spokesman for a product from NordicTrack called Ab Works. (Feel free to check it out on YouTube and enjoy the nineties splendor of my belly-button-level purple tights, midriff-baring shirt, and Flock of Seagulls haircut.)

The day I got that job, I distinctly remember having two sensations. On one hand, this was my dream, a real acting job (with lines!). On the other hand, I felt like I was going to throw up. I was paralyzed with fear—the fear of blowing it. Unfortunately, that feeling was ten times stronger than the elation of landing the gig. I couldn't eat. I couldn't sleep. I was a wreck. I contemplated backing out of the whole thing.

Thankfully, by that point in my life, I had a secret weapon, a mantra playing on a permanent loop in the back of my mind. That was probably the only reason I didn't bolt. Back then I may not have truly believed that mantra the way I do now, but just saying and thinking it helped me keep my eye on the prize.

*"Do your best and forget the rest."*

Some of you may have heard this one before—maybe because I say it all the time during my workouts. And with good reason! If you're looking for a way to help you turn your life around, to find success and happiness, you'll have a hard time finding seven better words. Let me tell you why.

## THE ANIMATED ADVENTURES OF YOUNG TONY HORTON

There's a reason why Disney hasn't come out with a Lil Tony Horton cartoon series. It would *not* be a fun show to watch. As a kid, I wasn't exactly a go-getter. The only thing I excelled at was excelling at nothing. I didn't do well in school. I got in trouble. My parents were in and out of the guidance counselor's office so often that they installed a revolving door with a brass plaque above it reading "For use by the parents of that delinquent Horton kid only."

My teachers and counselors told my parents time and again that I wasn't living up to my potential, that I wasn't willing to put in the work. And they were right. I didn't want to go anywhere. I didn't want to study. I didn't want to *do* anything. Why did I behave like this, you ask?

Because I was afraid.

I lived in constant fear. Fear of getting beaten up, fear of being made fun of, fear of being picked last for the team, fear of looking stupid, fear of getting a bad grade, fear of having to talk in front of more than two or three people at a time, fear of screwing something up, fear of showing up to school in my underpants.

Okay, I didn't really fear that underpants thing. But everything I did (or more important, didn't do) was painted with a sticky, sickly veneer of fear. When I went skiing, I was convinced I'd fall and, sure enough, I always fell. If I tried anything new, I went into it thinking I'd fail. And sure enough . . . thump.

Now, I'm not making excuses, but it's worth noting that I didn't have the easiest home life as a kid. I love my parents and I know they did the best they could, but they had a lot of challenges to deal with. My dad (Tony Sr.) was an army tank commander until I was five. When he shifted to civilian life, his job had him on the road Monday through Friday, traveling all over New England. So my mom was on her own five days a week raising my two sisters and me. I think she did an amazing job. The three of us turned out pretty darn well, all things considered. At the same time, life was hectic for both my parents—there was a lot of surviving without a lot of thriving going on—and us kids were influenced by that.

Because of my dad's jobs, we moved around a lot. To be exact: Rhode Island to Kentucky, to Hawaii, back to Rhode Island, to Connecticut, to upstate New York, and back to Connecticut—all before I was ten. Finally, when I was in fifth grade, we settled in Trumbull, Connecticut. By that point, fear had become my default emotion. I'd lived through being the new kid—and all the anxiety that came with it—too many times to remember. Like many new kids, I had the snot knocked out of me by my classmates every time I arrived at a new school (I also had my own revolving door to the nurse's office).

My senior year of high school, I joined the football team—a rare act of bravery for me. But when those Friday-night lights shone down on the field, I was sitting in the shadows on the bench. I was barely able to get in the game if we were up by twenty-five points. I didn't know it at the time, but the coaches just kept me around as a practice dummy. (In retrospect, that might have been because I had yet to learn how to do my best when it came to after-school practices.)

My dad, on the other hand, was always a champion sportsman. He was a three-sport captain—football, basketball, and baseball (he was an incredible pitcher)—and his dad, my grandfather, spent a lot of time making sure my father was the best.

Unfortunately his old-school, 1940s technique didn't leave much room for positive reinforcement. "Throw the ball fast and hard! Stop being an idiot!" As much as my father enjoyed sports and wanted to get better, I don't think he was a fan of that process. So when he had a son who played sports, he pretty much left me on my own. He tried to help me once in a while but I didn't respond well to constructive criticism. I know that he was doing the best he could . . . I just was so different from him. I got used to not wanting to be noticed, not wanting to stand out. Not wanting to try because of not wanting to fail.

## THE BIRTH OF A CATCHPHRASE

My lightbulb moment didn't come until years later, after I had decided to be a full-time trainer. (More about that in Law 3: Have a Plan. You're gonna love that chapter.) After that epiphany, I started finding myself in increasingly high-stakes situations—training celebrities, endorsing fitness gear, filming workouts, and pitching those workouts. Life became a constant stream of challenges that required me to get a handle on my fears.

Around that time, I started checking out the occasional self-help book or attending the odd weekend seminar. My life was improving, things were changing, but I knew I didn't have the tools to make the most of the opportunities that were coming my way. So I read the whole self-improvement canon: Keith Ellis, followed by Wayne Dyer, Gary Zukav, and Tony Robbins. Each and every book, every seminar, every mistake I made during that time helped me look inside myself and identify my fears so that I could build confidence and acquire the tools I needed to succeed.

Then came Don Miguel Ruiz's *The Four Agreements*, a quick read containing—you guessed it—four simple rules for living an excellent life. The fourth agreement particularly impressed me: "Do your best." Ruiz's point is that if you do the best job you can every time, no one—including yourself—can fault you for not trying. I thought this was incredibly wise. At the same time, it felt incomplete. For me, at least, it didn't clear away the static clouding my brain left behind by life's haters, the naysayers, and the football coaches. So I added something that made it sing for me.

Do your best *and forget the rest.*

"Do your best" means showing up and doing your best without being attached to the outcome. It means reality is not something you can manipulate. "Forget the rest" means you don't let the same things that used to get in your way, get in your way. It took years of trial and error, seminars and books, auditions, and, yes, *odd* jobs to put those two things together. Hopefully, this chapter makes that connection a little easier for you.

As a kid and in my early twenties, I didn't always take advantage of opportunities because I was afraid I wasn't ready. Before my lightbulb moment, I would have let the apprehension I feel about shooting a Pilates workout consume me. I probably wouldn't have had the guts to follow through (and if I had, I would have blown it).

But over the years, I've made a point of taking chances and gaining confidence in situations that would have scared me earlier. Equipped with "Do your best and forget the rest," I've come to learn that it doesn't matter whether you blow it or not. What's important is that you walk away with the knowledge that you gave it everything you had.

So, if this Pilates workout just doesn't work out—so what? Years ago, I stopped worrying about failure. I stopped making excuses. I stopped worrying about what people would think.

That's what got me and my purple spandex tights through that NordicTrack commercial. And today, when I'm faced with a seemingly insurmountable task, I try to do the same thing. Because the challenges are the best part of life. If you're not doing something scary, it probably isn't worth doing. Life should be about pushing yourself and moving into new territory.

## HOW TO PLAY TAG WITH NEW HATERS AND BLOCKERS

Some people fear change. They always did. If you look through history, there are two constants.

1. Some people fear change.
2. Those who can't overcome that fear fall by the wayside.

I'm talking about all the poor saps who feared fire, medicine, astronomy, democracy, and technology. If they'd prospered, we'd be living in a dark, flat world without voting rights, penicillin, or Pinterest.

But apparently, the descendants of these people didn't get the email memo (because they're scared of the Internet, I'm guessing) so they continue to refuse to adapt to the world as it changes and evolves around them. I called these people "New Haters."

New Hat•er /n(y)oo heyt-er/ *noun*. One who hates anything new.

I used to be a New Hater. I found ways to hate yoga before I tried it. Pilates is another example. Hated it before I had a clue what it was. Old dogs don't like new tricks and that's why old dogs get old faster than they need to. Although most people have come to terms with the fact that the world is round, New Haters still struggle with technology, fitness programs, nutritional advancements, politics, religion, equality, you name it. They're unhappy, frustrated, stuck people, so they keep trying to get by with old ideas that no longer serve them. Why take a risk on exotic fitness concepts or eat weird food like quinoa or kale? Why interact with people who might not see the world exactly like you do? Why read a book that might force you to see a new perspective? Why do any of these things when you can stick with the same old things you've been doing since before high school?

The answer to all these questions is that New Haters are afraid of change. I don't want to be completely dismissive of these people. After all, change can be a challenge. At the very least, it's uncomfortable. At the very most, it's flat-out terrifying. But still, it's what we need to embrace to do our best—and New Haters are afraid to do their best and forget the rest because it requires effort and dedication, which also bring the risk of failure. So when they see people adapting to and thriving in the brave new world around them, New Haters often lash out with criticism or dismissal. They judge, they condemn, they revile, they jest—in order to justify their own lack of progress. At this point, a New Hater becomes a "Blocker."

Block•er /blok-er/ *noun.* A New Hater who attempts to block your progress in order to justify their own inadequacies.

Odds are you have a Blocker or two in your life: a colleague, a boss, a friend, or a family member. When you make positive changes, they get uncomfortable—because they have to take a hard look at themselves. You were a certain way for a long time and maybe that Blocker has some of the same issues that you left behind. He or she carries a weight that's been lifted off your shoulders.

Other Blockers are complete strangers (and certain congressmen) loaded down with their own dogma or, even worse, by their own failure. They can't tolerate free spirits, productive people, happy people, people who think outside the box, people who want to change. Just like you, I've sparred with Blockers my entire life. Take P90X. People I didn't even know were waiting in line to say, "An extreme fitness program? You're never going to sell that! Why even bother doing it?"

Luckily, by the time I was developing the program, I had some serious fitness know-how under my belt, so dealing with Blockers wasn't an issue. In my younger years, the opinions of these people would have stifled me. I was too scared to trust myself. Nowadays it's different. I simply thank them for their opinion, make like Columbus, and hop on the *Niña*, *Pinta*, or *Santa María*, sailing off to the New World without them. Once you master that, the hard part of dealing with Blockers isn't ignoring them—it's not gloating when you prove them completely wrong.

If you listen to those people, odds are that you're as terrified of the world as they are, so do yourself a huge favor: Ditch the fear. Hate less and explore more. Go to that yoga class, eat that kale salad, smile at a stranger, listen to new ideas without that disapproving look on your face, and maybe, *just maybe*, life will get more fun and interesting.

And the next time a Blocker negs you, play a little game of TAG.

Take a deep breath. As you exhale, try to release your anger or frustration.

Acknowledge their opinion. If they feel heard, they'll probably leave you alone. Besides, most people are just looking to feel acknowledged in life—it's a simple (and free) gift to give them, and it may even help them see your point of view in the long run.

Go do your thing. It's the only way you'll discover how great your life can be.

The sad truth is that most people have a hard time learning this lesson—it's not as easy as it seems. Whether you're trying to invent an ice cream maker that uses only frozen bananas (It exists! I have one!), or you're just trying to get fit and healthy, or you're trying to reconnect with your spouse—it's your job to shine like some kind of crazy diamond. When you focus on the right direction, there's a much greater likelihood that you're going to stay with it—and succeed. You're bulletproof, as long as you do your best and forget the rest.

Part of my success in the fitness world is that I believe in the stuff I sell and I believe in myself. You can do the same. You may not think of yourself as the front man or front woman for a brand, but you are. You're the front man or front woman for You™. So forget everything. Forget the noise. Forget the Blockers. Just do your best at being you. You'll feel better. People will notice. They'll start coming out of the woodwork, then we'll all feel better together because misery may love company, but guess what? So do joy and success.

And that, my friends, is how this Big Picture thing works.

# FIND YOUR PURPOSE

*Everyone has his own specific vocation or mission in life; everyone must carry out a concrete assignment that demands fulfillment. Therein he cannot be replaced, nor can his life be repeated. Thus, everyone's task is unique as is his specific opportunity to implement it.*

—Viktor E. Frankl

We all have goals. They're a great way to make progress in life and keep moving forward in the right direction. Maybe you want to drop ten pounds, or do that 5K mud run, or get a raise, or get a date with that cute temp in the shipping department. These would qualify as short-term goals. They are all great motivators, but what happens once you reach them? Your short-term goal might be to sail out of the bay, but once you get there, you still have an entire ocean to contend with. And if you want to eventually sail to your favorite island, dock the boat, get out, and kick back with some coconut water (long-term goal), it's important that you also put some thought into why you jumped into a boat in the first place, and why you chose that particular island.

In other words, you need to find your purpose.

The French call it *raison d'être*, which loosely translates to "I smell magnificently of cheese." Okay, not really. It translates to "reason for being." Purpose is the reason you are. It's the deeper, driving force behind your goals. It's what moves you from here to there. How do you find it? Take your goal and look at it as part of the Big Picture, the view from sixty-four thousand feet. You know *what* you want to do, but *why* do you want to do it? How will your goal ripple across the rest of your life? Once you answer those questions, you're on your way to finding your purpose.

"Find my purpose?" you shout. "Tony, I'm lucky to find my car keys in the morning. I lose three socks every time I do laundry *and* I still have 'Missing Turtle' signs posted around the neighborhood in the hope that Mr. Sniffles will come back to his terrarium. And now you expect me to find my *purpose*?"

I understand. It sounds like a big job—but you can do it. After all, once you find a purpose, finding everything else gets much easier. That includes your keys, your socks, and Mr. Sniffles.

Here's a hint to help you get started: *Your purpose probably has something to do with having a better life.* For many people, the first "purpose" that comes to mind has to do with money, vanity, reputation, or material stuff. Forget about that garbage! It's all smoke and mirrors. Looking good in a bathing suit is a nice feeling, and driving a fancy car is fun, and having people think you're cool is flattering, but the thrill of those things subsides in a nanosecond, and you're left with nowhere to go. And, besides, when those kinds of goals are your main focus, it becomes destructive. You lose perspective. Maybe you wake up one day and decide there's no such thing as "too skinny" and you start treating your body in unhealthy ways. Or you stop caring about your financial commitments in the pursuit of the latest Thing and end up in a pile of credit card debt . No matter how you slice it, a shallow purpose isn't going to get you from point A to point B. It gets you from point A to point A and $\frac{1}{10}$.

They say that about 3 percent of the people on Earth live in bliss. So what the hell are the other 97 percent doing? Maybe they're spending too much time on ME, ME, ME! (By "me, me me," I mean "them, them, them," of course.) I'm not saying that your purpose should be to save the planet. However, I'm the first to admit that our planet could use a little saving. And one reason is that a big hunk of the human race treats itself horribly. They're overweight, stressed, depressed, and repressed. When you treat yourself badly, it becomes difficult to survive. And when you're barely getting by, it's pretty difficult to identify a sense of purpose larger than putting one foot in front of the other. And it's even harder to work up the energy to make strides toward your goals.

There's no doubt that taking care of yourself physically can help you with almost any purpose. When you feel better, you accomplish more—and that's not just some motto I got from a bumper sticker. A recent study out of Brigham Young University shows that people with poor diets suffered a 66 percent loss of workplace productivity. People who didn't exercise regularly lost 50 percent of their productivity. The numbers don't lie: Taking care of yourself enables you to be more productive—and that means you'll get more out of life.

Your brain, your heart, your lungs, your muscles, they're all interconnected. When you're physically healthy, there's a much greater likelihood that you'll see the world with more clarity. Which makes it a lot easier to understand your purpose. Once you do, you'll have a better chance of accomplishing it. Even if your purpose is Tibetan throat singing, you'll be able to hold your breath a lot longer when your lungs are working at 100 percent capacity. You see, even if you decide your purpose has nothing to do with fitness, it still has *everything* to do with fitness.

I know this all sounds a little esoteric, so let me give you a concrete example of purpose in action: my friend Jeremy Yost.

When I met Jeremy in 2010, he blew my mind. It was at a Beachbody Coach Summit and he was a Challenge winner, meaning he kicked butt and the company noticed, so he was there to collect his award.

When he first walked up to me, I saw him as just a normal, clean-cut, super-fit dude. (We get a lot of those wandering around at Beachbody gigs.) Then he showed me a photo of how he looked just one year before. My eyes almost popped out of my head, cartoon-cat-style. "Old" Jeremy was the sorriest-looking 370 pounds of humanity I'd ever seen. (Sorry, Jeremy. You know I love you, buddy.) If a picture tells a thousand words, 999 of those words were "miserable." I was riveted. How the hell did *that* guy turn into *this* guy?

I had to get into Jeremy's head. I needed to know what made him tick. What could motivate someone back to health after traveling so far down such a dark path? For the rest of the night, I pushed him for intel. Then I invited him to my beach workout the next morning, and we had a second round of interrogation. Still, I needed to know more. It took months of conversations before it clicked. Thanks to Jeremy, I saw firsthand how the Big Picture can pull anyone from the brink of self-destruction, can make even the most strung-out carb tweaker put down the Cheetos. Jeremy Yost turned his life around because he found his purpose.

# THE (NOT SO) TRAGIC TALE OF JEREMY YOST

Jeremy started out as everybody's all-American. In his Kentucky high school, he played football and baseball and he wrestled. I'm guessing he also had a Camaro and dated the head of the cheerleading squad, but we've never really discussed that. Anyway, like many of us, his exercise level slowed down in college and he soon saw signs of his upcoming struggles—a little pudge here, a subtle ache there—but he ignored them. "I kind of had it under control," he says with a shrug. After all, it was just a couple of pounds, right?

But after he got married and landed a job in corporate America, the wheels fell off completely. "I guess over time I had developed this mind-set that, because of work stress and because I gave it my all each day, I could reward myself through meals and just not being active," Jeremy explains. "It got way out of hand."

To make matters worse, Jeremy had broken his ankle playing football in high school. The pounds that his pizza and pasta habit packed onto his frame made it all the harder for him to get around on that ankle, let alone exercise with it. Soon he found himself at 370 pounds. He got to the point where he had to sit and watch his wife mow the lawn and do household chores. (I know, that sounds appealing for some guys, but I'm being serious here.) "I used my sheer size as an excuse," Jeremy says. "What am I going to do with my ankle and my size? It's not like I could go out, run a mile, and start doing something."

His tipping point finally came when he volunteered to help coach his sons Chase and Nolan's wrestling team. Here's how he told it to me:

When my boys started wrestling, I couldn't participate, I couldn't help, I couldn't really even coach. My son Chase was a five-year-old 45-pound kid; it's not like a 370-pound dad can get down on the ground and work with him.

My friend Tim was also coaching the team—he's in his fifties, in great shape. One day, we were driving to a tournament and he told me just that past week he had buried one of his friends who was only in his forties—the guy had kids. He said, "If you don't change your ways you're going to do the same thing to your boys."

Then he went on to say, "Your wife's young, your kids are young, they're going to move on without you. Are you confident that the guy that's going to replace you is going to do as good a job raising your boys as you would?"

I couldn't escape that. When I was 370, you can't be that size and not get in uncomfortable situations all the time. You get stared at. It's like a constant daze of self-consciousness. I would take my kids to the water park and take my shirt off and I knew everyone was looking at me. Up until this point I was able to run away from all those uncomfortable moments and find my safe haven, my couch. But after he said that, I couldn't escape, I couldn't forget it. That hit me right in my heart. It was like a light switch. At that moment, it wasn't "Am I going to be successful?" It was "I have no option."

That was when Jeremy found his purpose: his family. Jeremy's purpose became to make choices and do things that would enable him to be the best father and husband he could be.

"I would think, 'If I don't do my workout today I could die

tomorrow.' It just became so black-and-white. Every decision, every time I went to the kitchen, every time my alarm went off at four o'clock in the morning for my workout, it was do it or die," he says.

A couple of weeks into his journey, Jeremy made a "Why and Why Not" list to help him stay focused on his purpose. "I'd been thinking about all the reasons why I couldn't be successful but I hadn't put enough effort into thinking about why I should be successful," he reasoned.

Here's his list:

WHY CHANGE:

For my kids
For my wife
For me—I am worth it!
So I can walk pain-free (ankle)
To walk in a room and not be self-conscious
To meet someone new and not think about being overweight
To be able to take care of things around the house
To wear clothes that fit right and feel good
To enjoy buying new clothes and to never go into a big & tall store again
To take the kids to the pool and enjoy myself
To set an example to my kids so they won't have to go through the same pain
So that I won't avoid people
To improve my work life
To improve my energy
To know my kids as adults
To not be a sad story of a father leaving his wife and kids

WHY NOT CHANGE:

It's easier
It's convenient
Eating a big unhealthy meal is something I could look forward to
I deserve it
Everyone else seems to be able to eat what they want

I love this approach. On one side, Jeremy had a beautiful long list of reasons why. On the other side, he had a short, crappy list of reasons why not. (And did you happen to notice what those first two "Why Not" reasons have in common? Here's a clue: It begins with an *f* and rhymes with "beer.") It's as though the answer was already in his brain. He just needed to take a moment, sit down with pen and paper, and write it all down so he could see it in black and white.

## WHAT'S YOUR PURPOSE?

I don't know about you, but looking forward to knowing your kids as adults is a lot more enticing to me than looking forward to a bowl of Penne à la Porky Pig at Olive Garden. The Jeremy I met in 2010, the one living his purpose, agreed with me. "I think where a lot of people miss the boat when they set their goals is they don't wrap any emotion around it," he says. "It's easy to say 'I want to lose weight' or 'I want to get in that dress,' but they're missing the whole boat in terms of the emotional side of it. It's your emotions, your attitude, your deeper purpose, that's going to drive change."

Thanks to that mind-set, Jeremy is now more than able to get down on the mat and pin his two sons regularly; he's also looking forward to the day that they turn the tables on dad. "I want to see them win state championships."

In turn, his kids have also been able to adopt a whole new perspective. Before, their friends would hassle them about how fat their dad was. Now they want to hang out with him. They look up to him because of all the cool things he can do. In turn, they talk to their dads—many of them armchair quarterbacks not too far off from the old Jeremy—and say, "Hey, Mr. Yost can do it, how come you're not doing it?" Just like that, Jeremy has an influence not only on his kids, but also on his kids' friends, and his kids' friends' parents. All because a good friend instilled a little purpose into him when he needed it most.

Whether or not they're in good physical shape, a lot of people are like the old Jeremy. They're stuck. They can't see the forest for the trees because they don't even know why they're in the woods or which way they're headed. So many people suffer from lack of purpose. They're in survival mode 24/7. From the moment they wake till the second their head hits the pillow, they're on autopilot, and the idea of changing course is not only scary—it feels impossible.

But flying on autopilot isn't doing your best—it's not even taking active control of your journey. It's sitting back and letting something or someone else make the decisions for you. It's hiding behind false priorities (I'm too busy) and limitations (my ankle hurts). It's essential to wake up, take control of the joystick, and keep your eye on the proverbial prize. Your purpose should be your mantra, your mission statement. Think about what your purpose is for a minute—take a look at the "Picking a Purpose Quiz" on page 21 if you need help with that. When you're done, grab a pen and paper and write your purpose down. In fact, I want you to write it in this very book.

Here's the perfect space to do that:

**HELLO**
MY PURPOSE IS

Now make a copy of that and put it somewhere prominent. Stick it on your fridge. Tape it to your bathroom mirror. Use it as your screen saver. Get it tattooed on your butt. Get T-shirts printed and give them to the people you see every day. I don't care what you do, as long as it helps you remember your purpose.

Next, I want you to do exactly what Jeremy did: make a pro/con list, or in this case, a list of the reasons why you should take steps to follow your purpose, and a list of reasons why you shouldn't take those steps. (Go ahead, I'll wait.)

Now compare those two lists. I'm betting that list 1 is a lot longer and more compelling than list 2 (and if it's not . . . complete the quiz below immediately). Now look at list 2. How many of those reasons are based on fear? Cross them out. How many are false priorities and perceived limitations? Cross those out, too. How many do you have left? Are any of them actually good, honest, valid reasons to not pursue your purpose?

That's what I thought.

Nobody said there'd be a quiz! What the heck!?!

Relax. You're not getting graded. (You already earned an A+ just by picking up this book!) And while there are no right or wrong answers, there are revealing ones; these questions will help you dig a little deeper and make sure that the purpose you have in mind is the right purpose for you. That it's the purpose that will lead you somewhere you want to go.

1. How will this purpose serve me? How will this serve the people around me?
2. How will having this purpose impact my life in five years? Ten? Fifteen?
3. How will this purpose empower me to be healthier/happier/stronger/better?
4. Will this purpose serve me for life, or is it a short-term goal?
5. Will this purpose benefit me physically, emotionally, and mentally?
6. Is this my purpose, or a purpose someone else has assigned me?

## BABY STEPS ON THE WAY TO WORLD DOMINATION

Purpose is crucial, but your end goal can't be the only marker you strive for. On your journey, it's absolutely imperative that you smell the roses. Let's say that your purpose is world domination. It'll happen if you really want it to, but it might take a while and it can get pretty depressing if every morning you wake up and realize you haven't even dominated the mess in your apartment, let alone the entire planet. Always keep an eye on your purpose, but along the way, take time to appreciate small achievements that indicate progress (maybe you conquered cleaning the kitchen or the guest bedroom?). Doing that makes it much easier to keep moving forward.

Some days, it may seem like you haven't achieved anything. That's where Law 1 comes in handy. Ask yourself this: Today, did I do my best and forget the rest? If the answer is yes, then congratulations, my friend; you've achieved something.

Appreciating small achievements is especially simple when it comes to health and fitness goals, because most improvements are either quantifiable or tangible. Has your range of motion improved? Has your blood pressure improved? Can you do more reps at the gym? Have you lost inches? Did that guy really just whistle at you? As I said earlier, superficial stuff shouldn't be your focus, but it can make for a set of convenient benchmarks along the way.

This holds true for any goal you have in life. Maybe you're working toward a college degree but completion is years away. Every time you finish a course, revel in it. Or pick up the textbooks you had to read when you started. A year ago, they probably read like Latin, right? Now I bet they make complete sense. Nice work! *Veni, vidi, vici!*

While you're reveling in your achievements, be careful not to focus too much on any one particular marker at the expense of the Big Picture. For example, I mentioned measuring inches, but sometimes inches can be a huge demotivator when you focus on them too much—and you're not losing any. Body fat percentages, numbers on the scale, and inches lost don't always tell the whole story of a fitness transformation. Maybe you're gaining muscle mass as you burn fat or maybe the intensity of your workouts has temporarily triggered water weight gain thanks to an annoying (but useful) stress hormone called cortisol, so you're not seeing progress with your tape measure. Using just one indicator doesn't always reveal how hard you're working, not to mention how much better you feel. Same goes with those college courses—maybe you got a B when you wanted an A, or a C when you wanted a B. Of course all of that matters, but grades shouldn't be your only focus—are you learning a lot? Is doing the coursework fulfilling the criteria for your sense of purpose? Are you enjoying the class-work and the people you meet? Then a B might be just fine.

## FAILURE: THE NEW AWESOME

There's nothing wrong with failing. In fact, failure needs a new name. "Failure" should be renamed "awesome." Everyone loves awesome. I know this because anything of value nowadays is described as *awesome*! ("Nowadays" is a term that guys like me in their fifties use to distinguish the present from the "olden days," but I'm getting off topic.) Most folks think of failure as the opposite of success, but I beg to differ.

It's like what Winston Churchill said: "Success consists of going from failure to failure without loss of enthusiasm." Failure and success are Siamese twins; they don't exist without each other. There's no way around it. The problem with the word "failure" is that it connotes that you're a loser—and losers don't succeed or win or get the girl (or guy or pie or pot of gold or whatever it is you want to get). As a result, many people would rather play it safe, not take chances, not explore, and never, ever stick their neck out and actually *try*.

I was firmly "anti-failure" for half my life, and what did it get me? Not much. No adventures, no experiences, no learning, and no real success. Most people don't realize that failure is the key to joy, happiness, and growth. If you're afraid to fail, then you'll never expose yourself to opportunities for success. On the other hand, if you view failure as awesome, then you'll be open to trying things—and falling on your face, screwing up, making mistakes, and blowing it once in a while. Sucking at something every once in a while is how you achieve greatness in the long run.

## WHAT'S TONY HORTON'S PURPOSE?

Why, I thought you'd never ask!

There are a bunch of smaller reasons why I do the things I do: energy, enthusiasm, excitement, joy, mental acuity—the list goes on and on. I want to be fit and healthy so that I can have adventures and meet amazing people. I want several more decades of good use out of this body. (It's the only one I've got!) As a fitness role model, I want to talk my talk and walk my walk.

I could go on all day with those smaller reasons, but that wouldn't explain my raison d'être. I do what I do because there was a kid once who played college football. He was a huge lineman, whose purpose it was to move other guys out of the way so smaller guys could run around him and gain yards. But when he didn't make the pros, his purpose was gone. He was just a giant kid in horrible shape.

Then he found P90X and started working out. Recently, I met him at a ski lodge, where he told me he'd lost 130 pounds and showed me a video on his phone. It was him, a six-foot-six former lineman, doing a front flip off a cat track on a snowboard.

In a way, I'm the guy who helped him do that. I mean, he did it himself, but I got to help. A few decades back, I made the changes I needed to make in order to live a better life. Because I did that, my lineman friend was able to get his life back in order, too. I get to meet a lot of people who have similar stories, and those are the best moments for me, knowing that something I did could help somebody else live up to their potential.

My purpose is to help other people find their purpose.

*It takes as much energy to wish as it does to plan.*

—ELEANOR ROOSEVELT

The first time Tom Petty called me, I hung up on him.

Well, technically, my roommate, Bob, hung up on him. We were living in a small two-bedroom apartment in Santa Monica. I was just getting started as a trainer and Tom had been given my name from another client, music producer Harlan Goodman. So one day the phone rang and Bob picked up. A voice on the other end drawled, "Hi, it's Tom Petty. I want to talk to Tony Horton."

Bob put the phone to his chest. "This guy says he's Tom Petty. I think it's John," he said, referring to a friend of ours who was a chronic practical joker.

"Yeah, right, Tom Petty is calling me? No way!" I told Bob to hang up the phone.

Bob did just that. A minute later, the phone rang again. Bob picked it up. "Who is this?" he barked.

"Hi, ah, I think I got hung up on?" said Mr. Petty, who, being Tom Petty and all, probably wasn't used to being hung up on. "My name is Tom Petty. I'm a friend of Harlan's."

Bob looked at me. He was starting to believe the caller. "Give me the phone," I said. "John? Nice try, dude."

"No, it's *Tom Petty*," the voice on the other end corrected me. "Oh, crap," I mouthed to Bob. "This guy calling himself Tom Petty might actually be Tom Petty!"

Lucky for me, Tom Petty has a sense of humor, so the next day we started the process of getting him fit and ready for his next tour. But I bet you're asking, *How does that happen? Grammy-winning rock stars don't just randomly call fledgling personal trainers out of the blue.* A little serendipity, kismet, and Harlan's results, all mixed together, I suppose. I had trained a guy, who knew a guy, who happened to be Tom Petty. Dumb luck mixed with good timing, maybe.

Whatever it was, it was a huge turning point for me. It opened my eyes to two things. First, it's important to always be nice to people because you never know who might know rock stars who want to get in shape. Second, if I was going to succeed after having an opportunity like this dropped into my lap, I'd need to bring my A-game going forward.

Being introduced to Tom didn't guarantee that I would be successful. It was, however, a very clear opportunity to create success for myself. It was a sign, a calling, a twenty-foot-tall neon billboard alongside the Tony Horton Expressway telling me that, if I played my cards right, I might be able to parlay this personal training gig into a pretty cool career. But in order to do that, I had to do something I'd never contemplated before: I needed to decide on a goal (see Law 2: Find Your Purpose), plot a course in a new direction, and strategize.

In other words, I needed a plan.

## REBEL WITHOUT A PLAN

When I left the University of Rhode Island my senior year in the spring of 1980, several credits short of graduating, my grades were less than awesome. It was a definite low point. My friends were all graduating. The people I hung out with, drank too much beer with, and played Frisbee with were now going off to get married, start new jobs, and do something with their degrees. It turns out that when they weren't goofing off with me, they were actually *making plans* for the future. Futures with less Frisbee and more foresight.

I, on the other hand, was living day to day, afraid to take a risk or make a wrong turn. The future was a daunting thing and, as I may have mentioned once or twice, I was living a life in perpetual fear. What was coming next? I didn't know and I didn't want to know! If my life had a sound track, it would have been the theme from *Jaws*.

So when Bob called me one day and asked me if I wanted to jump in the car and head to California, I figured, "Why not?" I'd always liked acting. Maybe I could make something of myself in Hollywood. Besides, someone else was basically making the decision for me—how much risk was involved in that? So without hesitation I said, "Yeah." I dropped the bomb on my stunned parents and, with four hundred dollars in my pocket, headed for the West Coast.

By Colorado, I was broke.

Fortunately, while I didn't have a plan, I did have the ability to find my way out of an imaginary box. You see, I had the foresight to take a few pantomime classes in school because you never know when you're going to need to walk an invisible dog or drink an invisible beer. So I busted out my mime gear: black pants, black shirt, black vest, black hat, and the white mime makeup. In a day and a half I made about $125, enough to pay for food and gas to get me to Huntington Beach, California.

From there, I enjoyed the life of a beach bum, hitting the sand and sea every day to play more Frisbee, and hitting the clubs five to seven nights a week. I quickly scouted out the best happy hour buffets to pillage pigs in a blanket and fried shrimp. I was getting by with little or no exercise, and eating cheap (or free) food. No wonder I wasn't thriving. A lousy diet and little sleep from staying out all night have a tendency to suck the motivation right out of you—not to mention the ability to set goals and make smart choices.

To pay the rent, I did (almost) whatever it took. I waited tables, worked at clothing stores, go-go-danced. You read that right; $23.50 an hour to do the robot was a lot of money for me back then. I even made furniture. (Yup, furniture. I was lucky enough to sell a few pieces to a Big Nationwide Furniture Retailer with locations in a mall near you . . . so think twice before you throw out that ratty pine bookshelf or end table you've had since the Reagan administration. It might be a collector's item.)

When things were really bad I had to bust out the mime gear once in a while, which was humbling, to say the least. I'd go to the Santa Monica Pier or into Westwood near the University of California, Los Angeles, where kids would often find it amusing to steal money from my hat or heckle me. Street performance is fun when you don't need the money, but to be on the street performing for food money in front of drunk college kids took the fun right out of it. I just wanted to be left in peace inside my giant, invisible wad of bubble gum.

Being broke and hungry taught me to be inventive and creative, but that's about it.

I wasn't doing my best—though I was definitely forgetting the rest. The only sense of purpose I had was about my acting career. I was attending classes regularly and even landed a commercial agent. One day he said to me, "If you want to work in this town you've got to get rid of that belly and put some muscle on those arms." So with what little money I could scrape up, I joined a gym.

This was 1983, and gyms weren't on every street corner the way they are now. There were these things called "aerobics classes," and the equipment! Lat pull and leg extension machines, squat machines, and abdominal machines. It looked like a torture chamber, except the inquisitors were wearing neon spandex.

I followed the routine that the rest of the guys did: You worked on your chest for an hour and a half, pedaled on the stationary bike for forty-five minutes, and went down to the tanning booth to bronze your muscles (and accelerate your cancer risk!). Sometimes we'd break things up with an aerobics class, which consisted of three guys in a roomful of bouncing women (about as close to heaven as I could get at that point in my life). It had nothing to do with fast twitch, slow twitch, kinetic chain, or athletic performance. It was just getting the six-pack, getting the pecs, getting the biceps.

But still, it turned out that I had a knack for it, and soon opportunity came a-knockin'. Even though I was still lacking in both the ambition and guts departments, my friends were starting to establish careers. My friend John (the practical joker) was making a name for himself as a writer and helped me land a job as a personal assistant for a high-powered producer. One day, her associate producer, Harlan, said to me, "Wow, you're in pretty good shape. You think you can help me get like that?"

When I first started training Harlan I had no idea what I was doing. I basically had him do the same routine I did at the gym. But it was working for him, and unbeknownst to me, it was all about to pay off in a life-changing way. Because one day while Harlan was walking down the hallway of a Hollywood talent office, he bumped into his old friend Tom Petty.

"Wow, Harlan, you look fantastic. What are you doing? I'm going on tour soon and I need to get in shape," said Tom. (Or at least I'm guessing he said something along those lines. I have no idea. I wasn't there.)

So Harlan gave Tom my number, Tom called me, I hung up on him, and he called back, and I got the gig.

Here's where the plan comes in: This wasn't just any client. There was a lot at stake—a lot of money and other people's reputations and livelihoods. These people were all counting on me, trusting that I knew what the hell I was doing. I had to make sure that I didn't injure this guy. Up until this point, I'd been lazy about everything I did. I was a lazy actor. I was a lazy trainer. That wasn't going to work anymore. It's not that my other clients didn't matter—because they did—but it felt like a lot more responsibility had been dropped in my lap because I was dealing with a guy who made his living getting onstage and entertaining thousands of people. If I screwed up, he wouldn't be able to do that.

On the other hand, if I became the guy who whipped him into shape, some high-profile people would notice. I knew that if this worked out, instead of waiting for the occasional door to open for me, I could start opening them myself.

I had to make a decision. Did I want to continue barely getting by, surviving on instinct and scrappiness, or did I want to commit to something bigger? I dialed up my intensity and cut back on the shenanigans. A little less nightclubbing, corn-dog eating, and Frisbee playing. A little more reading up on exercise and nutrition, working out every day, and becoming more disciplined.

And my efforts showed. I began to attract more clients, including more celebrities—and those clients saw results. Soon it became a full-time job. I didn't have to commit to waiting tables anymore. I didn't have to commit to the bartender gig anymore. The only thing I needed to commit to was my plan—and it felt great.

And that, my friends, is the story of how Tom Petty got fit, and how I embarked on my Big Picture journey.

## THE PLAN AND YOU

I admit that my situation was pretty unique—I had made a lot of bad decisions and just happened to be rescued by being in the right place at the right time. Unless you have a time machine and bear a very striking resemblance to me, your experience will be different. But the lesson I learned all those years ago is universal: When life comes knocking, don't be afraid to answer the door (or the phone). What does that mean for you on a practical level? It means getting your life in order and getting your plan together.

This sounds more complicated than it is; formulating your plan is simply a matter of deciding what you want, then plotting a course to get there. Start with the simple things. Commit to eight hours of sleep each night. Cut back on caffeine, alcohol, and sugar. Surround yourself with people you can trust. Exercise! I know I sound like a broken record, but this is really, really important. Get your body in a healthy place, and the rest will start to make sense.

And here's a little trick: If you know where you want to be but can't figure out how to get there, start with your goal and *work backward*. Steve Edwards is vice president of fitness and nutrition at Beachbody, the company that creates, markets, and distributes P90X and all my other fitness programs. He plays a pivotal role in helping me plan my programs. When we build a new fitness series, we don't just throw a bunch of workouts into a salad bowl. We look at the big-picture, bird's-eye view of the whole program. Once we know the results that we want to deliver (in other words, the purpose of the plan), we can break it down, step by step, into a series of manageable chunks. In other words, we commit to the endgame and work backward from there. Or as Steve says, "To get from point A to point Z, start at point Z. You start at the goal and then you back up from that goal to the start."

This method of planning works for both short- and long-term goals; just be sure to keep your purpose in focus when you formulate your plan. Lose twenty pounds, spend more time with your girlfriend, learn how to play "Stairway to Heaven" on the guitar— whatever it is. As Steve puts it, "The best way to figure out what you *need* to do is to first figure out what you *want* to do." And you can only know what you want to do if you've taken the time to discover your purpose.

# SCHEDULE, SCHEDULE, SCHEDULE

Scheduling creates accountability; it gets you organized and keeps you honest. Planning in advance also saves time. Yes, I know, it seems like a hassle, sitting down for thirty minutes on Sunday afternoon to plot out your strategy for the week, whether it pertains to exercise, food, balancing kids with work, or completing your toothpick replica of the Taj Majal. But trust me, that "goats that sound like humans screaming" video you want to watch on You-Tube will wait. Once you create a schedule, it will make sticking to your plan a hell of a lot easier.

I learned this lesson thanks to my fitness schedule. Back when I started taking my career seriously, I realized that if I didn't make myself workout-accountable, I'd probably return to the land of twenty-four-hour party people. How could I preach the importance of fitness if I wasn't walking the talk? So I started recording my exercise schedule. To this day, I write down and schedule all my workouts in advance. After I do them, I x them out. At the end of the month, I add up all the x's. My goal (since back in my Petty days) has been a minimum of 22 workouts a month—that's 264 a year with 101 days off—at most.

Whatever supplies you need to make your schedule—go get them and do it. Take a trip down to Office Supply Super Store Plus and buy a big, beautiful calendar. Put it up where you'll see it every day—on the bathroom mirror, the refrigerator, or right on the inside of your front door if you have to. I have a large desk calendar that stares back at me every day. A lot of people use their iPhones or computers to schedule and that's okay, too, but there's something about seeing the task at hand in front of me, literally in black-and-white, that makes it seem all the more urgent. If you don't know what you're doing and when you're doing it, every day, your plan is toast. It amazes me how many people wake up in the morning with no idea of exactly *how* they're going to take care of business that day.

We're pretty good at scheduling when to go to the movies, scheduling when to go on a date, or figuring out the order in which to watch our favorite shows on the DVR. But we find ourselves perpetually trying to *squeeze in* the things that will actually help us, the things that constitute progress toward our plans. The "fit it in whenever" approach might work for a little while, but it never survives in the long run. If you make it a point to schedule in advance, your chances of success will skyrocket. My trusty calendar has kept me honest for decades. Without it . . . I'm lost. With it I'm organized, committed, and successful.

At the same time that it's important to be organized and maintain some kind of structure, it's also essential to make that structure flexible. Build it out of pine, not concrete. Be prepared to adapt your plan. When I first moved to California, I was going to be an actor, but like John Lennon said, "Life is what happens to you when you're busy making other plans." I saw the writing on the wall, and I shifted my plan and redirected my passion into being a trainer. If you have a larger purpose in place, it will be clear whether or not shifts in your plan are okay. The same is true for plans involving short-term goals. You'll find that as long as you keep one eye on your purpose or your goal, on the "point Z" that Steve was talking about before, then changing your plan should be just fine. In other words, write your plan down, but write it in pencil. Erasers are your friends on the road to success.

But look out; planning can be addictive once you see how well it works. Soon you'll be accomplishing all kinds of big things using this super-powerful weapon. In no time, success will come calling. When it does, take it from me: Don't hang up.

## SCHEDULING NUTRITION (OR, PLANNING FOR SUCCESS, ONE BITE AT A TIME)

Back in my twenties, if you asked me what I planned to eat for the day, I'd respond, "Whatcha got?" Today I'm a little pickier. Because I'm a flexitarian—meaning I have a largely plant-based diet with the occasional organic, sustainable animal protein—it varies, with the exception of the fact that 90 percent of my food choices are clean (no processed stuff) and healthy. I talk the talk; I walk the walk; I eat the eat (you know what I mean).

I can't stress enough how much health and fitness need to be part of your plan. Your body and the brain are your most basic tools for any project. Their health is critical to your success. if you focus too much on other goals and let your health fall by the way-side, you will eventually derail your goals—or at the very least, have some really ugly setbacks.

With that in mind, menu planning and food journaling are a must. Planning up front helps you organize cooking times and grocery shopping trips. Food journaling means writing down what you eat every day so that you can look back at performance peaks and sags, with an eye for what foods might have influenced those shifts. For example, if you felt like you were on top of the world on Wednesday, with energy to spare, a productive mood, and a brain firing on all cylinders, chances are you fueled your body with some good nutrients and drank plenty of water all day. On the flip side, if on Friday you had a lousy day with a splitting headache, low energy, and a terrible attitude, a peek at your journal might indicate that your lackluster performance had something to do with your participation in a Thursday-night happy hour, and the ensuing Friday-morning grease-bomb breakfast.

Now, even with all the scheduling in the world, life puts you in situations where you're stuck eating junk. Layovers at airports, road trip pit stops, Thanksgiving at Aunt Olga's house—you know the drill. But, frankly, how often does that really happen? At least 90 percent of the time, we have control over what we eat and how much we move. We stock our own refrigerators, plan our own meals, pack our own lunch boxes, and pick the restaurants we want to try (or at least make our own choices off the menu someone else picked). We create time to work out, select our workouts, know when it's time to work out and when it's time to rest. So don't worry about that troublesome 10 percent. When you absolutely *can't* follow the plan, that's okay. Just make sure to get back on the plan ASAP and see Law 1: Do Your Best and Forget the Rest.

## Five Days in the Life of Tony Horton's Stomach

Since people ask me all the time about my diet, here are five days from my very own food journal. Be careful. It's going to make your mouth water.

### MONDAY:

| | |
|---|---|
| POST-WORKOUT | protein shake with egg white protein, blueberries and strawberries, raw cashews, coconut water, and almond milk |
| BREAKFAST | oatmeal with berries, ground chia seeds, and granola |

| LUNCH | mixed green salad with roasted beets and grilled chicken; bowl of chicken and mushroom paprika soup |
|---|---|
| SNACK | carrot chips and hummus |
| DINNER | quinoa pasta with arugula and basil pesto, grilled chicken and baked garlic asparagus |

Notes on the day: In terms of a "typical" day of eating for me, there are two separate scenarios. The "I'm home for a while and things are kind of normal" scenario and the "I'm on the road and nothing's normal" scenario. Today's meal plan is the former. I'm home, there's food in the house, and my workload isn't too crazy, so I can be strategic about my eating.

## TUESDAY

| POST-WORKOUT | protein shake with egg white protein, blueberries and strawberries, raw cashews, coconut water, and almond milk |
|---|---|
| BREAKFAST | scrambled eggs with fresh salsa and avocado; yogurt with berries and granola |
| LUNCH | vegetable chili |
| SNACK | Greek yogurt with strawberries |
| DINNER | mixed green salad with grilled salmon, mashed sweet potatoes, saffron rice, and steamed veggies. |
| DESSERT | handful of organic, dark-chocolate-covered almonds |

## WEDNESDAY:

| POST-WORKOUT | protein shake with egg white protein, blueberries and strawberries, raw cashews, coconut water, and almond milk |
|---|---|
| BREAKFAST | oatmeal with berries, ground chia seeds, and granola |
| LUNCH | vegetable curry with brown rice |

| SNACK | cucumber slices with hummus |
| DINNER | rotisserie chicken with mixed steamed veggies |
| DESSERT | handful of organic, dark-chocolate-covered almonds |

Notes on the day: Busted! Chocolate two nights in a row! Dessert is my nemesis. I consume it based on two things. The first is caloric output. I've worked hard today, so I can afford a few extra calories. The second is just cuz I wanna.

I'm on the 90/10 plan, meaning 90 percent of what I eat is clean, but some days it's more like 80/20 and other days it's 100/0. I'm perfectly okay with the occasional indulgence because long-term success comes from having a certain amount of discipline without ever feeling deprived.

## THURSDAY

| POST-WORKOUT | protein shake with egg white protein, blueberries and strawberries, raw cashews, coconut water, and almond milk |
| BREAKFAST | oatmeal with berries and ground chia seeds; Greek yogurt with berries and granola |
| SNACK | Greek yogurt with blueberries |
| SNACK | leftover vegetable and quinoa frittata |
| SNACK | handful of raw cashews |
| DINNER | cedar plank salmon with steamed broccoli and fingerling potatoes |

Notes on the day: Why three snacks in a row? Because I don't cook. When my girlfriend Shawna is working, she sometimes doesn't have time to make meals, so I look to healthy snacks as a substitute for a healthy meal. It's not perfect, but it's better than going hungry.

## FRIDAY:

**POST-WORKOUT**  protein shake with egg white protein, blueberries and strawberries, raw cashews, coconut water, and almond milk

**BREAKFAST**  three eggs over easy topped with ratatouille and sliced avocado

**LUNCH**  three-bean soup

**SNACK**  protein bar

**DINNER**  quinoa pasta lasagna with ground buffalo and vegetables (no cheese)

**DESSERT**  Coconut milk ice cream with frozen blueberries

Notes on the day: Today I had an all-day photo shoot at Beachbody, thus the need for the protein bar—or as I call it, "emergency food." Far too many people see protein/energy/meal replacement bars as a substitute for a healthy meal. My answer to that is "Not a shot." Not even close. However, if you are in a pinch and need some quick nutrition, find one that's low in sugar and unpronounceable ingredients, high in fiber, and organic. Keep a few around to break out in case of emergency. Otherwise, you're better off with whole food quick snacks such as fruit, nuts, and seeds.

## ADVICE FROM THE EXPERTS:

### Beachbody CEO Carl Daikeler

Few people have had the impact on my life that Carl Daikeler has. I first started working with him as his trainer. Things were going great, but then I got a gig as a trainer on a movie called *The 13th Warrior*, so I needed to leave him on his own for three months. I wrote him out a plan and went on my way.

Typically in those situations, by the time I get back, my client hasn't made much progress. But when I returned, Carl was ripped! I couldn't believe it. "What the hell did you do?" I asked. He shrugged his bulging deltoids. "I just did what you and I talked about."

I knew then that this was a man who understood a plan.

A couple of years later, he came to me with an idea to create a video workout for his new company Product Partners (which would eventually become Beachbody), so we powwowed and came up with Great Abs Guaranteed. It was a hit, so then we took it even further and created a more comprehensive program called Power 90. That was a bigger hit, so then we came up with a more hard-core program called P90X.

Although Carl claims not to have a "dogma" about planning, he's sure doing something right, so I asked for his thoughts on this law. Pretty great stuff, if you ask me . . .


**TONY:** Having worked with you for a while, I know that a "Carl plan" is always flexible. It seems like you improvise based on what you see going on around you.

**CARL:** I'm not a buttoned-up, organized guy, I'm a creative guy. And you want to turn a creative guy off? Tell him to write a plan. A different word for writing a "plan" is defining a clear "objective," and once you put an objective or goal in front of a creative guy with ambition, it's on.

Take P90X. If you put "I want to be absolutely ripped in ninety days" as the goal, there have to be steps to get there. So either you can guess and maybe you'll get there, or you can plug into certain proven steps that will get you there. The only dogma of it is to be fiercely committed to taking action every day. That doesn't mean the plan is set in stone. And I'll be honest with myself about what's working and what's not working.

Now take the creation of P90X. The goal was to create something that was as close to the authentic gym experience without headbands and Jane Fonda bodysuits people expected in a workout video. We wanted something that would feel as authentic as working out in the gym without having to traipse to the gym, if that's a word, "traipse"?

**TONY:** Yeah, it's a word.

**CARL:** Good, so that was the goal—the vision—and we knew what the process was from doing Power 90, so that is the makings of a plan. Every stage of the development process, we would look at results and next steps against the goal and weigh it.

For instance the very first gym set that our director proposed was this high-tech reflective floor, a white *Tron* sort of thing. Cool, but not that authentic, gritty concept that I wanted. We started to look at locations around town, boxing rings, gyms in basements, and we just decided to build it ourselves with exposed brick, moldy lockers, and an industrial fan in the background. That fits the vision, right?

**TONY:** Absolutely, but what lesson can we take away from that?

**CARL:** Well, you can never go on autopilot with a plan and that's what I think so many people take for granted. If you're building a house you've got plans for it: there are all these variables of materials, weather, geographical surveys, all these factors that you don't know until you're in the midst of the building, that you need to take into account. So the most important thing is that you don't just "set it and forget it" with a plan.

Just like when you drive a car. You don't just jump in your car and point it in the right direction. You have to actually make constant little adjustments in steering, with traffic lights and other traffic, to get yourself to your final destination.

**TONY:** But life doesn't have a final destination. Well, technically it does, but leading up to that, it's important to continually set bigger goals toward your purpose.

**CARL:** I didn't have a plan to make Beachbody a billion-dollar company, but once I got to $100 million I started to say, "Hey, we can make a plan, we can actually get to $300 million" and so on. You're constantly reacting and that, I think, is what's fun about having a plan. You look at what you've achieved and what you want to achieve and then you move the markers to the next level and you put new designs in place for what you can then achieve.

It's the opposite of people who live waiting for life to come to them. Then you're just a victim or you're a lottery winner, so I choose to live life with a plan or a goal. I lay out the steps to get there and then assess them constantly. But usually I only get a clear snapshot of my plan when I look in the rearview mirror and see what I did.

**TONY:** I'm hearing a lot of wisdom in there. One: You need to be flexible and adapt. Two: It doesn't hurt to throw things against the wall and see what sticks. Three: If something in your past has worked, honor that. Four: Check in all the time.

**CARL:** I think that's good. Also—and it's very cliché—but everybody says enjoy the journey. And that's really true, too.

# LAW 4
===

## VARIETY IS THE SPICE OF . . . EVERYTHING

---

*Variety's the very spice of life, that gives it all its flavor.*

—WILLIAM COWPER

Now that you have some idea of where you want to go and how you're going to get there, you're going to need some serious tools to help you on the journey. So say hello to my three little friends: Shemp, Curly, and Moe. No, wait, that's not right. Kim, Khloe, and Kourtney? Nope, definitely not. Variety, consistency, and intensity? That's it! These three laws are my "Big Three," the cornerstones of living a better life.

I've been pushing the Big Three as the keys to any successful health and fitness plan for years, but I'm here to tell you that these laws go way beyond eating and exercise. In fact, you can apply them to any career goal, relationship, project, or any other purpose in your life. Feel like making toast for breakfast? Do it with variety, consistency, and intensity and that'll be the best piece of toast you've ever had.

I know that sounds silly (*me*, silly?) but I'm completely serious. Let's break it down. By using variety, you'll try new, healthy bread options and you're bound to discover something delicious. (I'm a sprouted-grains guy myself.) By implementing consistency, you'll make sure that toast is perfect every time. Don't walk away while it's in the toaster and accidentally burn it. Make sure it's perfectly golden brown and still warm when you bite into it. Finally, exercise your intensity. Don't read the paper while mindlessly shoving toast down your gullet or eat it in two quick bites as you rush around getting ready for the day. Put it on a plate, sit down, and chew it. Savor it. Taste all the different components of your toast. Taking your time when you eat also helps you to not overeat, because you realize when you're getting full and stop eating instead of gobbling down a bunch of other junk that you don't need.

See what just happened? You made a fulfilling experience out of one of the world's most mundane activities. Imagine what'll happen when you apply these laws to larger projects.

## SPICE IT UP

We'll get to Consistency and Intensity in a bit, but in this chapter, we're going to take a closer look at Variety. Long story short, variety ensures that you mix things up. If you want to be stuck less in life, then you need to be open-minded. If your belief system hasn't changed since the last century, it's going to be a problem—because the world has.

Spontaneity and creativity are cornerstones of variety. They're the reason why things change and improve, the reason why you have options. The reason that cars, computers, and phones look different and work better than they did ten years ago is that designers and engineers harnessed their creativity and decided to try something new. The reason skateboarders get serious air is because a bunch of punks in the seventies got tired of skating on flat surfaces, so one day some guy spontaneously experimented with a little vertical variety. Athletes move faster, push harder, and jump higher because they constantly challenge themselves in different, unique, and innovative ways. They take advantage of planned and unexpected opportunities for growth and explore them to the max.

Stay curious and creative and think outside the box. What piques your interest? Have you explored it yet? If not, that's today's assignment. (Provided, of course, it's legal. Otherwise, I don't want to know about it.)

## THINK CREATIVELY ABOUT CREATIVITY

People often misunderstand creativity as a talent that's used solely for artistic pursuits like painting, sculpture, or interpretive dance. Nothing could be further from the truth. Creativity is an essential skill for success in any type of activity. It's about seeing problems from different angles in pursuit of a solution. It's about trying new recipes to discover ways to enjoy foods you previously thought you hated. It's about walking your dog a different route so that you discover some beautiful little park that you didn't even know was there.

I don't paint or sculpt (I plead the Fifth on interpretive dance), but I'm deeply creative with my work and the rest of my life.

Curiosity is about having an open mind—and it's a wonderful thing. Once you've mastered that, creativity is the next step. It's about not being afraid to share that creative, open mind with the world.

## BE A ONE-MAN (OR -WOMAN) VARIETY SHOW

I learned the importance of variety firsthand as a trainer working with celebrities. Technically, working with big shots isn't all that different from working with anyone else. We all have the same muscles, the same limbs, and the same excuses not to do cardio this morning. But here's one big difference: If your client loses interest and quits, a long chain of very influential people will quickly brand you as "boring" and make sure everyone in their circle knows it. When I was starting out in the training business, I felt a lot of pressure not to let anyone down. I needed to deliver results and stay employed.

So, as you may have guessed, I took a deep breath, did my best, and forgot the rest. And part of my "best" was getting creative and including variety in the workouts I created. After all, I'd spent a lifetime using my imagination to survive; now I had an opportunity to use it to thrive. I brought in as many variables as I could. For example, Tom Petty loved hitting the heavy bag, so I focused on that, teaching him spin kicks, spin punches, push kicks, and crotch kicks (ouch!).

Working with celebrities was planting the seeds for P90X and my other fitness programs, not just in terms of variety, but also in terms of home fitness. Sometimes the gyms I designed for these folks were the only places they could really work out. Some rock stars simply can't go for a walk or a run in the neighborhood. They can't bring their entire entourage to protect them from being swarmed at a 5K. So they need to find a technique that serves their purpose and meets their specific circumstances.

As a trainer, the best way to help your clients progress is to keep them interested. And the best way to keep them interested? Variety. Most people go to gyms because they're looking for variety—lots of different machines, a slew of classes, and a bunch of people to work out with. Training people in their own homes taught me how to inject variety into a workout because there were no machines, classes, or crowds to fall back on. I had to be spontaneous and look for fun, innovative ways to make things interesting with the tools I had at my disposal. I had to create variety out of almost nothing if I wanted my clients to stick with the program and get results.

Admittedly, there was also a selfish aspect to this whole thing. At the time, we didn't know what we do today about exercise science. Trainers like me were all doing the same thing—weights and resistance and intervals and cardio—but that was it. And that got old for me really quickly. (Stephen Stills has been amazing in concert, but try watching him on a treadmill for forty-five minutes, the high point being when I got to check his heart rate.)

The point is, I needed the variety as much as my clients did. "What's that you say, Tom? You like the punching and kicking part? Sure, we can do more of that!" So I'd to go to a bunch of martial arts classes and learn from people that were really good— and I'd have a great time doing it. Then I'd hang up heavy bags at clients' houses so they would have another way of doing cardio. And I'd be able to kick the bag around as well, as opposed to standing there and watching them pedal that stationary bike.

I didn't know it at the time, but in my pursuit of variety, I was progressing past weight training and cardio. I was starting to put together a program of interval exercises and flexibility exercises and core exercises. My creativity was leading me to innovate and discover new things. I was always on the lookout for spontaneous opportunities—to be aware of what was unfolding in front of me (in this case, paying close attention to my clients' progress and enthusiasm) and to respond to it in a way that kept the momentum going.

## THE VARIETY BALANCING ACT

Variety isn't just about adding zing to your life. It's also about making sure you cover all your bases. I stress this to anyone doing my workouts. When it comes to exercise, a big part of variety means you're constantly working different muscle groups and different bodily systems to keep your body in balance. If everything works equally in your body, it's easier for everything to work right. It's the basic principle of cross training. Doing new and different things promotes adaptation and wards off plateaus. When you add variety, change is inevitable. When you skip variety, you're just riding the Plateau Express to Injury Town (a lesser-known prequel to *Murder on the Orient Express*).

The classic example of this is strength training and yoga. On one side, you have your typical weight lifter who has been lifting, squatting, benching, and curling for twenty years, but has completely forsaken stretching. Sure, he has massive biceps, but he's incredibly tight. His hamstrings are like two steel cables stretched to the snapping point. All that pressure is pulling down his spine, so it's just a matter of time before he develops lower back issues. And if he wants to try any sport requiring range of motion, he can forget about it.

One the other hand, there's the yoga veteran who can turn her body into a pretzel with the ease that most of us *eat* a pretzel (a whole-grain spelt pretzel, of course), but whose strength training consists of lifting up her Styrofoam yoga blocks. Her problem is that there's not much protecting those hypermobile, superflexible muscles, so the first time she lands on her knee wrong, pop! It's off to the orthopedic surgeon.

And that doesn't even include cardiovascular fitness! Suffice it to say that when the zombies attack, muscle boy and yoga girl aren't going to outrun anything. They're both undead lunch (although the weight lifter will probably be a little tough).

On the other hand, if the weight lifter increased his range of motion with a little yoga, he'd be able to work his muscles deeper. If the yoga practitioner did a little strength training, she'd have the endurance to hold poses longer. Add a little cardio, and both might outrun the zombies and live longer, healthier lives.

You can plug that same lesson into almost any aspect of your life. Let's say there's a Type-A intern who's so consumed by her job that she doesn't see the Big Picture. Yes, she works hard—and she always gets the job done—but she doesn't care who she has to bulldoze to do that. Because of this, she doesn't have many fans in the office, so when her internship wraps up, well, she's a hard worker and all, but no one wants to have Little Miss Bridge-Burner in their department!

Now let's say that, in the same company, there's a laid-back Type-B middle manager. His employees love him because his mellow demeanor makes him fairly adept at dealing with conflict, but he has no fire in his belly. Opportunity comes and goes and he never grabs for it. So when promotions come up, he is always passed over because the powers that be want someone who will move mountains to get the job done. Eventually the company downsizes, eliminating middle management. Bye-bye, Mr. Laid Back.

But what if Type-A Girl had taken the occasional deep breath and been sensitive to the people around her? What if Type-B Dude had pointed out his conflict resolution track record to his superior and pushed for a promotion? The answer is that they'd probably both still be employed.

(Now that I write this, I'm thinking that these two couples should meet so they can help each other. It might be a love connection, thanks to T. Ho's Variety Dating Service.)

## WHEN IT'S TIME TO TRY SOMETHING NEW

Curiosity is a key reason I've been able to sustain a high level of fitness all these years. If I see something that looks fun and challenging, I try it. If it doesn't ring my chimes, I move on to something else. And when I find something I like, that doesn't mean I'm going to get it tattooed across my chest. (Besides, it's a long list, all the things I like. My pecs are big, but they aren't that big.)

When it comes to my hobbies and interests as well as my Big Picture goals, I make a point of staying open-minded and paying attention to shifts in my tastes or needs. Too many people hold on too tightly to strategies, thoughts, or activities that don't work for them anymore. You want to avoid that.

Think about it: They. Don't. Work. If your television broke, would you keep it? If your car died, would you park it in the backyard, fill it with dirt, and use it as a planter? If your phone stopped working, would you just stop calling people? Of course not! If any of these things broke and were no longer of service to you, you would fix them or get new versions of them. If you have an activity, habit, or ritual that's no longer serving you, why on earth would you keep at it?

## ARE YOU BEING SERVED?

Technically, it should be pretty obvious when what you're doing no longer works for you. Unfortunately, it's not. Life is packed with so many should-dos, shouldn't-dos, could-dos, can't-dos, want-to-dos, and just plain doo-doo that sometimes it's tough to see the forest for the serviceable trees.

To help you, I've come up with a quick test to determine the serviceability of your activity. Whenever you answer "yes" to one of these questions, add or subtract the points indicated.

1. Do you enjoy doing it in the moment? (Add 5 points.)
2. Do you look forward to doing it? (Add 2 points.)
3. Do you talk positively about it to others? (Add 1 point.)
4. Is it hurting you? (Subtract 10 points.)
5. Is it hurting others? (Subtract 10 points.)
6. Are you benefiting from it physically, mentally, or emotionally? (Add 5 points.)

**3 OR LESS POINTS**    You've got yourself a toxic activity, my friend. Time to ditch it.

**4–8 POINTS**    You're probably fine to keep doing this, but I wouldn't make it a priority.

**9 OR MORE POINTS**    Keep it up! (And let me know about it because I want to try it, too.)

You know it's time to change things when you hear yourself saying things like "I'm burned out," "This isn't fun anymore," or "I'm not getting better at this." You could be suffering from a temporary bout of mind babble, or maybe it's your heart telling you that it's time to move on. Only you know the difference. Don't do something just because everyone else is doing it. Figure out what keeps you in the game, even if it's very different from what others think you need.

I've met people who struggle with their weight but say they won't eat veggies because they're "meat and potatoes" people. Or people who are unhappy with their fitness level but say they don't have time for exercise (but they do seem to have time to surf the Internet or watch TV). I'm not telling you that there's a one-size-fits-all solution to everyone's problems or that there's one enlightened path to everyone's success. What I am telling you is that if the thing you're doing isn't working, open your eyes to the thousands of other options you have out there and try a few of them. Introduce variety into your life.

Look at technology, nutrition, fashion, hairstyles, ways to relax, or colors to paint your fingernails. There are thousands of ways to change, upgrade, or reinvent yourself. When you're willing to embrace variety, life is better, more interesting, and more fun.

It's easy to fall into the tried-and-true "if it ain't broke, don't fix it" mind-set. And sure, there are some oldies but goodies in life that are worth preserving. (I'm all for current trends in art, but guess what's hanging over my mantelpiece? A painting by Theodor Geisel—aka Dr. Seuss. Old-school and awesome.) But there's a fine line between honoring tradition and holding on to the past. In almost every category of life, there's the old way and the new way. Oil and gas versus wind and solar. Fast food versus healthy, whole foods. Weightlifting and cardio only versus functional core fitness that incorporates speed, balance, and flexibility.

Young people who don't know about the old, dated ways of doing things automatically jump into the most modern version of life. On the other hand, the older folks get, the more resistant to change they tend to become, even if the old model of life doesn't work anymore. I see it all the time when I ski—people my age or older are still using skinny skis that make them work harder than they need to just to make their way down the mountain. Things become outdated because someone has found better ways to do things. Sometimes it's the financial, mental, or emotional cost of change that deters folks from upgrading their lives, but most often it's plain stubbornness. They say, "This is what I know, and this is how I think, so this is how it is," even if it doesn't work and even if they're stuck and unhappy.

Opening yourself up to new options means changing, and changing means being vulnerable, and people don't like being vulnerable. You might say, "Better safe than sorry," but from my perspective it looks more like "Better safe than better." So take a hard look at your hobbies, habits, possessions, thoughts, actions. If any of them are broken, hindering your progress, not good enough, or just generally not serving you—try something new. Try a little variety.

## FROM LITTLE THINGS, BIG THINGS GROW

I, personally, do a lot of exploring via my fitness because I know that a lifetime of fitness is achievable when you explore new roads to health. The workout I did this morning? First time ever. Those reps, the order, the range of motion—all different from the previous workout. I knew I was going to do chest and back, but that was it. I just threw twenty-four moves into a blender and went for it.

I understand that not everyone feels comfortable making things up on the fly. And structure is important—routines and habits are the building blocks of any successful plan (remember, this is the guy who has a paper calendar on his desk). But there's always room for variety within structure. I know people who absolutely, categorically need to eat oatmeal every morning. Oatmeal, raisins, and a little honey. It fills them up, energizes them, and keeps them regular.

That's great. It's "heart healthy." But how about using dried cranberries tomorrow instead of raisins? I know, I know. Wacky! Once you've adapted to that massive paradigm shift, try fresh fruit. Maybe replace the honey with blackstrap molasses. Then try replacing the oats with Greek yogurt. See what happened there? Variety isn't always a giant change all at once. Sometimes it's a series of smaller changes. You can use that method across your entire life. If you want to transition to your dream career, you don't need to quit the job that's paying the rent. Instead, maybe start by taking night classes. It's like what songwriter Paul Kelly sings: "From little things, big things grow."

## VARIETY ISN'T ALWAYS PRETTY

One of the challenges of trying new things is taking a risk. Variety requires you to push yourself outside your comfort zone, which means that you're not always going to come out the gate looking awesome. In fact, you're probably going to fumble and fall quite a few times. Who cares? How are you going to live your purpose if you don't face your fears? How are you going to get better if you don't *get better*?

I know that it's important to put myself in positions where I'm not king of the mountain if I want to progress. Some people say it's lonely at the top. I think it's pretty boring up there, too. I take a sprinting class with Olympic runner Malachi Davis at the UCLA track. No way am I the alpha in that pack. Those guys are fast! I get a little nervous and intimidated each time I meet them at the track, but that's okay because I learn so much from them. I can't let ego get in the way of getting better, stronger, faster—not to mention meeting new and interesting people. The first time I went, I announced my disclaimer: "Hey, I know I'm Mr. Trainer Guy, but this is new to me. I'm not going to injure myself trying to prove something. I'm going to do my best and work within my abilities." After that, it became a fun day of hanging out with really cool people and trying something different.

## BALANCING OUTSIDE YOUR COMFORT ZONE

A few summers ago, I found myself at a garden party. I was losing interest in the small talk, so I stepped outside for some fresh air and discovered that the hosts had set up a slackline, which is basically a really taut nylon strap (also known as webbing) suspended between two poles or trees a few feet off the ground. The idea is to use your balance to stand on it, walk across it, or do circus tricks on it. I hopped on and fell right off. This was clearly not something I was going to pick up quickly. When I was younger, that would have been the end of it—I wouldn't have wanted to look silly or stupid. I used to be petrified of anything I wasn't good at.

But on this particular evening, my buddy Ted and I spent the next hour falling off that slackline over and over again. I embraced the challenge in part because falling down repeatedly was more appealing than the small talk at that party. Driving home that night, I knew this was something I wanted to master. I bought one and put it up in my backyard. It took me three weeks, and I slowly got better.

When ski season started, a funny thing happened when I hit the slopes on day one: My skiing had improved dramatically. Balance has never been my strong suit, but all that time working on the slackline was paying off in dividends. Embracing the moment and seizing the opportunity to introduce a little variety in one part of my life helped me to be stronger and more successful in another, seemingly unconnected part of my life.

And that's the trick. Don't focus on the pitches you know you can knock out of the park. Instead, swing at the curveballs. That's where growth comes from—not just in the activity you're doing, but also in dozens of other ways you weren't expecting.

Now I have two slacklines in my backyard and a third one that I travel with. Something that was completely off the radar to me is now an indispensable part of my weekly routine. And that just happened . . . it happened because I wasn't feeling chatty at a party, and I was looking for some variety. The key is to get outside your comfort zone and do things that are different from what you're used to. If you suck, who cares? You can either keep trying until you improve, or learn a valuable lesson and move on. At the same time, don't forget to keep doing the stuff you are good at and enjoy. The alchemy will be fantastic.

## MAKE IT INTERESTING

Once you peel back all the other benefits of variety, at its core you'll find this simple truth: Variety makes life interesting. You may be one of those rare people who are perfectly content to cycle through a series of push-ups and crunches, then hit the treadmill, day in and day out. I admire you, but I don't really want to hang out with you. I bet you also spend Friday nights organizing your sock drawer.

The rest of us need to shake it up. Keep trying new things so that you can find things that excite you. You can include variety in any of your chosen activities. In yoga, you can try Hatha, Iyengar, hot yoga . . . there's even Acroyoga you can do with a partner! There's variety within martial arts. You can go from tai chi all the way up to mixed martial arts, and everything in between. If you're a runner, you can do intervals and sprints, run indoors and outdoors; if you're a cyclist, you can do single-track time trials one day and tear through a national park on a mountain bike the next. So even if you really, really like what you do and don't want to stray too far from the ranch, don't be afraid to shake it up a little. That applies to the rest of your life, too. If the only veggie you can stomach is cauliflower, give broccoli a try. If all you ever watch are Matt Damon movies, throw some Jason Statham in there. (What do you have to lose beside two hours of your life?)

And you won't just be helping your fitness and nutrition (or increasing Jason Statham's royalty payments) when you do this. Every time you do something new, your brain creates new neural pathways. Something as simple as a new route to work or a switched-up morning routine is actually a form of exercise for your noggin.

It's important to keep in mind that checking out something new doesn't mean that you're committing to it. Just because you say "om" once in a yoga class doesn't mean you have to build a yurt in your backyard. In fact, I've hosted events where I'll do some yoga, and it surprises me how many people are too afraid or offended to om. They weren't raised with an om. What is an om?

Is it some kind of crazy Taoist, yogi-culty thing? No, man, it's two letters that help you relax and enjoy your yoga practice.

In fact, let's all say it together now. Ready? One, two, three . . . "Ooooooooommmmmm."

Did you say it long and loud? Not so bad, right? Now, if you look in the back of the book, there's a document I want you to sign that will release all your earthly wealth to ME!

Kidding! The point is, committing to the om can help improve your yoga practice. The same principle applies to your Big Picture plan—when you shake things up, add in some variety, and look at things differently, you not only stay interested, you also prevent yourself from getting stuck in a rut. In fitness, when you do the same workout every day for months on end, you get hurt, you get bored, and you stop seeing results. In life, if you plod through each day with the same strategy and an inflexible game plan, you're basically running in place—you're not getting any closer to your goals. And if you're mindlessly slogging through your life without any variety, creativity, or spontaneity, chances are you've lost sight of your purpose, too.

## VARIETY IN THE KITCHEN

I don't believe in a dogmatic approach to eating. Food is fuel, and there's a lot of biology at play when it comes to what diet works best for you. For example, some folks are so into eating paleo—avoiding grains, legumes, and dairy—that even when they don't feel right, or they're tired all the time, they stick to their plan. Other people embrace a plant-based diet and go vegan for twenty years, only to wake up one day and, like me, realize something is wrong. They feel run-down. They don't recover from workouts as fast as they used to. When that happens, it's essential to adapt—and the best way to adapt is to add variety to your diet.

The nutrients that fuel us are wildly complicated. First you have your carbs, protein, and fat. Then you have vitamins and minerals. Next you have phytonutrients (nutrients from plants) and zoonutrients (nutrients from animal sources). And bringing up the rear, all kinds of enzymes, probiotics, and other organic bits and pieces, the roles of which scientists are still trying to figure out. On the one hand, it seems like every day there's a new study coming out about how some super food is now super-*duper*, or some food we previously thought to be awful might not be so bad after all.

On the other hand, you have the human body, which is every bit as complicated as all that stuff we put into it. And even if you completely understand your body and how it reacts to your diet today, the same foods might not work for you tomorrow because, after all, as your body changes, so do its needs. My body thrived for years when I was a vegan. Then, one day, that style of eating longer worked for me.

Luckily, you don't need a Ph.D. in nutritional biology to sort this all out. In fact, you don't need to sort it out at all. The key is simple: Eat a variety of foods. The more varied your diet, the greater your chances of getting the right combination of nutrients to suit your needs.

For example, fruits and veggies get their color from phytonutrients. Anthocyanins give red cabbage, blueberries, and blackberries their blue or purple color. They're also a powerful antioxidant. Lycopene is the stuff that turns tomatoes and watermelons red. It's also been shown to increase longevity. Chlorophyll, which puts the "green" in leafy greens, is a great detoxifier. Garlic and onions are white thanks to allicin, which also has anti-inflammatory and antimicrobial properties. Are you seeing the trend here? All these nutrients help you in different ways, so it's important to eat the rainbow.

Variety is also a good way to avoid bad things. The omega-3 fatty acids in fish are important, but if you go crazy on the red snapper, you can have issues with heavy metals like mercury. On the other hand, organic, free-range chicken is a great protein source, but it doesn't pack the omega-3 wallop. So what if you mix it up? That way, you get regular, healthy protein, some omega-3s, and less mercury. Everyone wins. (Except the fish and the chicken, but let's not go there.)

If you're healthy, you feel good, you have energy, and you don't experience a lot of aches and pains, then you're probably managing quite nicely with your current plan, so go right ahead and stick with it. You may have found that magic combo, for now. But stay open to the idea that at some point, your body may be asking you for different nutrients—so be sure to listen to it! That's the way I eat, because just as it is with fitness, when it comes to nutrition, variety is the spice of life.

# LAW 5

## CONSISTENCY REIGNS SUPREME

*Sustaining an audience is hard. It demands a consistency of thought, of purpose, and of action over a long period of time.*

—BRUCE SPRINGSTEEN

On any given Sunday, if I'm not skiing, you'll find me just south of the Santa Monica Pier at the original Muscle Beach or on my backyard jungle gym. Both feature high bars, rings, tall and short ropes, slacklines, and parallel bars. (I added a pegboard and campus board to my outdoor gym.)

Once a week, I met a group of friends at the beach or at my place for a two-and-a-half-hour upper-body workout extravaganza. It all started over ten years ago, when P90X Bobby Stephenson and I would run two and a half miles to the beach and do rope climbing and dozens of push-ups, pull-ups, and dips. Then one day, this guy Chuck Gaylord joined the party, and everything went vertical. Our simple pull-up and dip workout morphed into "gymnastics for old guys." Handstands, flying plyometric dips, upside-down rope climbs, muscle-ups on the rings, and the occasional backflip became the norm. It's extreme, with a capital *X*. I love it and hate it at the same time. Which is why I love it.

One day a young guy showed up on the beach and politely asked if he could join us. I was dubious at first. After all, you've gotta be pretty tough to hang with this particular group of Sunday-smack-talking show-offs. Then I thought, Why not? Let's see what the kid's got.

With no further ado, he sauntered over to the pull-up bar and started hammering 'em out. And that was just the start! This kid could climb a rope like a monkey with his tail on fire. There was nothing he couldn't do. Finally, I spoke up because I was worried that the Navy SEALs were infiltrating our little group. "What's your name?" I asked him.

"My name's Sterling Purdy," he responded in a southern drawl.

"That's quite a name," I retorted, "and how come you're so strong?"

He grinned. He'd been waiting for that question. "Because of you, Tony." It turned out that Sterling had been doing my workouts for a while. He was on a business trip in San Diego and he'd driven a couple of hours up the coast in hopes of finding our little group and joining us for a real, live workout.

It was another beautiful reminder of my raison d'être.

## MEET MR. CONSISTENT

The story of Sterling Purdy is an epic ballad of consistency. Homer's *Odyssey* type of stuff. *Lord of the Consistent Rings.* He is a great example of the fact that transformation can be a bumpy road, but if you stick with it, if you do what you need to do every day, you'll get where you want to go.

Let's hop into the Wayback Machine and travel to the year 2004. NASA landed two rovers on Mars. Dubya won his second term as president. Britney Spears and Kevin Federline tied the knot, wearing matching tracksuits. And Sterling Purdy hit a personal low as he lost his job and took on a serious couch-surfing habit, packing 225 of (mostly) fat on his otherwise slight five-eight frame. His weight gain and lack of fitness had a devastating impact on his health. He found himself taking enough prescription drugs to fill every medicine cabinet in Graceland. "I was on high-blood-pressure medicine. I was on a low-testosterone medication. I'd had asthma my entire life, so I was on multiple asthma medications," Sterling told me. "I was on depression medicine, a blue pill—I don't remember the name of it—but I do remember it was hard to get off of. Honestly, I don't remember all the medications."

So Sterling decided to make a change. Unfortunately, for his first attempt, he didn't choose what's behind curtain A. Instead, he opted for curtain N, as in, "Not what Tony would have done." He started a low-carb diet and added a weight-loss medication to his nightly pill dosage. This strategy worked, briefly, but the moment he started eating a few carbs and went off the medication, he just gained the weight back. Furthermore, those quick-fix solutions did nothing to improve his medical conditions.

So he gave P90X a try. He was in pretty bad shape, so it took a few rounds, but he stayed consistent. "I just dredged my way through it over and over," he says. And when he'd had enough of those workouts (although I don't really understand how *anyone* could have enough of P90X), he added some variety. He stayed committed, but he substituted home workouts with sprint drills or long morning bike rides. He also changed his eating habits, stripping processed foods from his menu.

How did he stick with this plan every day? "It was definitely just being consistent and patient and knowing that the weight would come off eventually," he says. And the weight did come off. As it did, other things happened. "I felt so much better. And of course the healthier I got, the less medicines I needed to take."

Even without his mysterious, addictive blue pill, Sterling's mood soared. Exercise floods your brain with "feel-good" hormones called endorphins, so consistent workouts mean a consistently happy noggin. Furthermore, as John J. Ratey, M.D., points out in his breakthrough book, *Spark: The Revolutionary New Science of Exercise and the Brain* (which you'll find on Sterling's shelf, as well as mine), exercise doesn't just make you feel good by activating the hormones in your head, it makes you feel good *about yourself*—and so it should because you're challenging yourself. You're achieving something. "If you've been feeling down and you start to exercise and feel better, the sense that you're going to be OK and that you can count on yourself shifts your attitude," Ratey writes. In my opinion, you're not going to find a better self-esteem booster.

"When I'm exercising I'm just a different person," adds Sterling. "I'm happier when I'm working out and feel better about myself. My wife can attest to that."

When Sterling reached his goal weight, guess how he celebrated? He kept going, eventually hitting 7 percent body fat and becoming a lean, mean, rope-climbing machine. Where he could do five push-ups and maybe one or two pull-ups when he started, now he can pull off 150 to 160 pull-ups a day!

Of course, he doesn't always maintain that level of fitness—you don't really need to unless it's your job—but he remains consistent, eating right and working out regularly. As he puts it, "I like to think I practice consistency from all angles."

Good plan, Sterling.

## CONSISTENT ALL OVER

You've got to be consistent about being consistent. It should permeate every part of your life. Be consistent when you brush your teeth. Be consistent when you get eight hours of sleep at night. Be consistent about showing up to work or school on a regular basis. Be consistent when you follow the rules of the road. Be a consistent parent or spouse.

When you stop being consistent in any of those areas, you get into trouble. Stop brushing your teeth and flossing every day and you'll probably need a root canal. Stop following the rules of the road and you'll get a ticket. And consistency is important not only for you, but also for the people around you; being consistent in your relationships is key. An inconsistent worker creates more work for others. An inconsistent friend isn't really a friend. An inconsistent parent ends up with a troubled kid. Showing up on time, returning phone calls, being a good listener . . . these are all forms of consistency in life. While I'm not going to get too high-and-mighty by calling it a "moral imperative," consistency in your actions is a necessary part of being a good person and a productive member of society.

Take writing this book, for example. My collaborator, Denis, and I sat down and wrote it—not just every now and then, but consistently, most days, until it was done. No matter how much was on my plate, or his, we were consistent in our work. And while we worked on it, I stayed consistent in my message. I didn't come up with the 11 Laws one day and then try to write a detective novel the next. (Although it wouldn't be a bad idea. *Murder on the P90Xpress? The Bourne Consistency? The Da Vinci Core Synergistics?*)

The point is, no matter what, we kept the forward momentum going. We didn't sit still. In fact, "sitting still" is just about the worst thing you can do. It's the new "going backward." It's the ultimate metaphor for the way many people live their lives, sitting still on their couch, watching television; sitting still in their cars, zoning out the world; sitting still at work and blankly staring at a computer screen.

We need to do things that *propel us forward* for our families, our work, our health, and ourselves because that's how we grow and get better. It's how we live our Purpose and how we progress in our Plan; it's how we inch closer to realizing the Big Picture.

## BLOOD AND BREATH

But let's get back to the fitness thing for a second (sorry, can't help it). A simple way to think about consistency and its benefits is to use the most fundamental, basic units of our lives: blood and breath. If your blood stops flowing and/or you stop breathing, you will die (unless you're a vampire). Blood and breath are your body's way of being consistent for you, so it's important to return the favor and keep these systems working as smoothly as possible.

Even though your body regulates blood and breath automatically (how cool is that, by the way?), you can profoundly influence its ability to do that efficiently with diet and exercise. You can keep your blood vessels clear of plaque, your heart strong, and your lung capacity deep. When you don't support your body's automatic, consistent mechanisms, guess what? They become inconsistent. So when you don't eat nutrient-rich food and you spend more time being still than moving, you make it harder for your blood to pump and breath to flow. You begin to experience the effects of a less-than-consistent system, which can include heart disease, asthma, and lethargy, to name a few side effects. Your body can be consistent only when you're supporting its efforts.

When it comes to consistency in fitness, I always recommend a five- or six-day-a-week exercise habit. And by five or six, I don't mean three. Three days a week of "maintenance" doesn't exist. When you exercise three days a week, you develop what I call "exercise bipolar disorder." Sure, you're progressing those three days, but then you're falling back during the other four days off. There's no consistency, so your mind and body don't get into the habit of craving movement—you're just kind of in that mental state where "going to the gym" feels like a burden rather than a regular part of your day.

Inconsistent exercise is the life equivalent of driving across the country on surface streets. You're bound to hit stop signs, streetlights, detours, construction, weird guys wearing trash bags and tinfoil hats who want to wash your windows—you name it. Hell, there's not even anything good to listen to on the radio. You spend a ton of time with your foot on the brake, wondering why you're not getting anywhere, why you get sick all the time, why you're tired all day, why life is just plain blah.

That kind of trip sucks, so why not jump on the fitness freeway, drop the top, and get the wind in your hair? The consistent, six-days-a-week mentality and lifestyle will get you on the "open highway" to a better you. Your blood and breath need to move all seven days of the week. When you move your body just three of those days, you've left your heart and lungs yearning for more. Your absolute minimum should be four days. Five is pretty good. Six is ideal. Seven works, too, if you do it right.

Another benefit of thinking about consistency in terms of blood and breath is that, regardless of external benchmarks like pounds or inches lost, you know you're making a positive impact on your insides with every workout. Goals like number of reps, weight, range of motion, and intensity are important, of course, but thinking about all those variables can be overwhelming sometimes. If you just focus on making sure you're breathing deeply and moving blood through your body, then you're in the game. Even something as simple as walking briskly around the block gets your blood pumping and your breath flowing. When you're moving and it feels strenuous, you breathe deeper. When you breathe deeper, you inhale more oxygen. Your blood soaks up that $O_2$ and carries it, among other places, to your brain. Much like glucose, oxygen fuels your mental functions, so when you get plenty of it, you think and feel better—and that improved mood and clarity will transfer to everything you do.

## "DID YOU REALLY SAY SIX DAYS A WEEK?"

I can hear some of you out there beginning to panic. Relax; this is a free country, not the United States of Horton (yet). If you want to sit around all day, that's fine with me. But before you put on your XXL sweatpants and flop down on the couch with the remote, let me ask you some questions. Do you sleep every night? Eat every day? Shower (almost) every day? I'm going to assume you answered yes to all of those. Okay, then: What happens if you don't sleep for a few nights? Skip some meals? Go without showering for a week?

What happens isn't pretty. You end up a smelly, ravenous zombie. You feel terrible. You look like hell. But the moment you get some nutritious food in your stomach, the instant you step underneath that hot water, the second you wake up from a good night's rest, you feel revitalized and reenergized. *It's the same with consistent exercise.*

Here's another thing to consider: Exercising six days a week will obviously help you meet your fitness goals; but what may be less obvious is how a consistent fitness regimen will support your Big Picture goals. When you exercise consistently, you are repeating and reinforcing a new behavior pattern and creating a good habit. We all know that bad habits are easy to establish, but so are good ones, if you keep at it. It takes deliberate, conscientious effort at first, but once you've been consistent with a good habit for a while, it will simply become part of your lifestyle. When you establish a healthy exercise habit, it will become easier to establish other healthy habits. It's like having a pair of consistency training wheels. Your consistent nature will bleed out into other areas of your life.

- You'll eat healthier because your body will crave the nutrients it needs to get the most out of your workouts.
- Using exercise to cope with stress will give you enough distance to see problems from a new, healthier perspective.
- The realization that you can establish a new, healthy habit will inspire you to establish more beneficial habits in other aspects of your life.

When you adopt a fitness regimen that includes your weekly six workouts, you also begin to embody a philosophy that constantly reminds (and demands) you to take better care of yourself, not just on weekdays or weekends, but all the time. Case in point: Say you worked out a few hours ago. You're upbeat and feeling great, when all of the sudden you come across a Danish that's calling your name. You know that eating that sugar/fat bomb is going to undo all your hard work and make you feel like crap. What's more, when you're fit, your body awareness goes up, so junk food might still taste okay, but if you overindulge, look out! You'll really *feel* the brain fog, the malaise, and the lack of muscle recovery. These things may just be a way of life for unhealthy people, but for you, they'll be something you'll actively avoid.

For all these reasons, you're less likely to put it or any other food you don't need into your body. Slowly you'll begin to notice that your food choices will improve consistently; you'll avoid fried food and processed garbage loaded with fat, sugar, salt, and chemicals.

### FUN WITH HABIT FORMING

Another reason to exercise six days a week—or to do anything that's good for you as often as you can—is that repetition forms habit. When you repeat a new behavior consistently, over time that behavior becomes new learning—your brain develops new neural pathways that are reinforced each time you engage in that behavior. In other words, when you make a conscious effort to do something different— eat a salad for lunch, go through your email inbox first thing in the morning, take ten minutes to meditate in the evening—eventually, those behaviors become less conscious and less of an effort . . .

and more like a habit you just *do* without thinking twice about it. How long it takes to form a habit isn't entirely clear. The oft-quoted twenty-one days has never been proved. In truth, it depends on the person and the habit. But nobody denies that repetition is key to causing behaviors to become instinctive.

## THE EXERCISE DEVIL ON MY SHOULDER

Here's a dirty little secret: I don't get all that fired up about exercising most of the time.

Some people have the exercise bug; their motivation never wavers and nothing slows them down. I am not one of those people. After thirty years, you would think the desire for exercise would be automatic for me, but it's not. Mostly because of the three little voices in my head.

Voice number one is the halo-wearing, angelic Tony on my shoulder. He's my enthusiasm, my excitement, my desire to sweat and compete and feel good. He's my "Can't wait! Looking forward to it! Feeling strong! Let's get out there and kick some ass!" voice. I hear him about 21.35 percent of the time.

Voice number two is the red-horned, pitchfork-wielding Tony. "Oh my God, I can't believe I have to do this right now," he complains. "This is the very last thing I've ever wanted to do. Actually, maybe there's something on HBO right now and it'll never be on again and the DVR accidentally forgot to record it! Let's just have a chocolate chip cookie." He pipes up 35.4 percent of the time.

Voice three is the middle guy. He's the voice of consistency. He's effective, but he's about as exciting as a wet dishrag. "All right, here we go, yeah, yeah, going to train now. It's going to be okay," he says in a matter-of-fact voice. He's just there to figure out the most pleasant way to get through something I'm not all that into at the moment. He's talking about 43.25 percent of the time.

Luckily, I have democracy on my side. Angel Tony and the boring consistency guy add up to 64.6 percent, so they usually win. Devil Tony has launched an aggressive redistricting campaign in hopes of increasing his influence, but so far he hasn't made too many gains.

We all have those three voices—or maybe it's just me (uh-oh). Unfortunately, the consistent one tends to get ignored—probably because he's so boring—and without him, the angel doesn't stand a chance. So if you're sitting around waiting for him (or her) to overpower your devil voice so that you can effortlessly launch into whatever unpleasant task is at hand, it ain't gonna happen. That angel needs a little help. If you still can't seem to hear Mr. Consistency, go grab a voice recorder and recite the following:

"You have to do it, so just do it. Listen to the angel. I know he's kind of annoying, but it's the right thing to do. You'll be happier and healthier when you've done it."

Next time the devil's voice comes a-knockin', play that recording—and I'm not just talking about getting motivated to work out. I'm talking about motivation to do anything. For example, let's take your garage. No one *likes* cleaning the garage— and it's certainly not going to clean itself—but once it's tidy and organized, you can rest easy knowing it's not going to take you four hours to find the holiday ornaments next December. Or how about homework? Again, not exactly a festive activity, but if you don't study, you tend to fail—and I'm pretty sure that repeating tenth grade isn't part of your Plan, right?

So get busy!

Keep in mind that consistency doesn't just mean repetition. Do what you need to do, but whatever that is, it shouldn't be the exact same thing over and over. Not only will you get bored, but also it's a surefire formula for plateauing. Neither your body nor your mind will progress if it's running continually on the same loop. Doing the same exercise every day is just like reading the same book, eating the same meal, or hanging out with the same people every day. It's a guaranteed recipe for boredom and burnout.

## STAYING MOTIVATED ON THE CONSISTENCY FREEWAY

There are certain issues that rise to the surface when it comes to consistency. One of them is motivation. How does anyone sustain anything without being motivated? There are a million obstacles out there. We travel, get sick, get tired, and get discouraged. We work too hard, we undersleep, and we get stressed out. Like the bumper sticker says: "Shit happens." So what do we do about it? Sometimes it can be overwhelming.

Just like there are people who seem to effortlessly maintain an exercise regimen, we all know those folks for whom "quit" is a four-letter word. Who are these people that never quit? Are they some kind of advanced android race from a galaxy far, far away? What the hell makes them so special? Why are these robot people so consistent? What keeps them motivated?

The answer is that successful, consistent, and motivated folk have tricks to keep them going. We've already covered a few of them: Make a Plan you can stick to and hold yourself accountable to. Throw in some variety—keeping yourself interested goes a long way toward motivating you to do what you need to do. The biggest trick, though, is plugging into your Purpose and focusing on the rewards that come with following it. That alone should be enough motivation to keep you on track. If you have your eye on the prize, it's much easier to stay consistent.

Consistency may not be sexy or exciting, but there are no "cons" in consistency—just "pros." In fact, we should rename the word "*pro*sistency." (Someone get Noah Webster on the phone.) Improvement and growth occur when you do things repeatedly and often. Stopping and starting sporadically kills the momentum you need to succeed. Consistency keeps you in the game. I love it when people discover my fitness programs and hit them going 100 mph. I don't love it, however, when they crash, burn out, and quit. I'd rather they take their time and ease into an exercise regimen, even if it means starting smaller. Done consistently, moderate forms of exercise provide far better results than the occasional full-body pummeling.

The same rule applies for most aspects of your life. Some things, like quitting smoking, might require you to go cold turkey, but for the most part, baby steps are *the way to go*. The word for this is *gradualism*. It's the notion that several small, key shifts effect permanent, positive change better than one, sweeping one. It's a concept embraced by government, business, biology, linguistics, and basically anyone else who's smart, rich, or powerful. I don't know if you're rich or powerful, but I know you're smart, so why not give it a try? (And if you do, rich and powerful might just drop into your lap, too.)

If you want to take up meditation, you don't need to shave your head and move to a mountaintop temple. Start by getting into that lotus position for five minutes in the morning—every morning. If you want to give up caffeine, you don't need to deal with withdrawal headaches. Just reduce your intake by one less cup of coffee each day. When you're down to one cup, switch to green tea, then switch to herbal tea. If you want to have a more positive attitude, you're not going to shake your Charlie Brown ways overnight. Instead, make a point of saying one nice thing to someone every day, then two, then . . . you get the picture. Make a consistent Plan and stick to it.

## YOUR NEW BEST FRIEND OPIE

So how do you do this gradualism thing? It's simple. You just need a Plan. Follow this nifty little acronym, OPIE (Andy Griffith would have been proud), and you'll get the job done.

ONE PROJECT AT A TIME.   You may want a lot of change quickly, but if you pile it on, you're more likely to crash and burn, so pick one thing to start with (personally, I'd start with exercise) and go for it. Once you're happy with where you are, add the next project.

PARTITION THAT PROJECT.   A major shift can be overwhelming, so break your project into bite-size pieces. Maybe you want to run ten miles a day. Start with two, then five, then seven, then ten.

IGNORE YOUR SCREW-UPS.   You're going to mess up along the way. You're going to miss a workout, or "accidentally" eat half a sausage pizza. Don't use this as an excuse to quit. Own your mistake, get past it, and keep going.

EVALUATE YOUR PROJECT.   Check in periodically to make sure this project still works for you. Remember that ten-mile running goal? Does it make your knees hurt? If so, maybe it's time to abandon this pursuit and take up swimming or cycling.

# THE FINE ART OF BEING IMPERFECT

Sometimes the biggest obstacle to consistency has nothing to do with external factors. Some days, you just don't feel like you have what it takes to do what you need to do.

Do it anyway.

I don't care how you do it. I don't care if it's ugly. I don't care if you do it hard or slow. I don't care if you do it with a fox, or if you do it in a box, in a house, or with a mouse. Just get it done.

There are times when all you need to do is check the box and do the best you can. It's not always about hitting a home run. For example, I had a photo shoot where I needed to demonstrate a variety of exercises. It turned into a five-hour exercise marathon. On top of that, I thought a yoga class at the end of the day would be a wise idea.

The next day, I was trashed, but I had a shoulders and arms workout in the schedule. What to do? Blow it off or show up? I chose showing up and backing off by 25 percent. After all, choosing nothing gives you nothing, so what was there to lose?

And what a great learning experience it was. Even though I had to go through the motions for some parts of the workout, I actually surprised myself and others—I even squeaked out a few personal bests. I didn't go in trying to do that; I went in with the goal of just showing up and being consistent. And look at what happened when I took a risk. Growth.

The lesson learned here spreads across all aspects of life. "Bringing it" doesn't mean it has to be brought like LeBron James and Peyton Manning—they lose games and underperform too, don't forget. You don't need to solve every dilemma like Sherlock Holmes. You just need to show up. Perfectionists usually say "no" more often than they'll say "yes" because they're perfectionists. They don't want to do anything that will make them look bad—but that's a silly way to live. Fear of failure sets up ridiculous expectations and, ironically, actually sets you up for failure. Drop that philosophy like a bad habit. Some days are going to go well and some days are going to go horribly and some days you might expect to go horribly wrong and will surprise you by going well instead (and vice versa). You might be Wonder Woman one day and the Wicked Witch of the West the next. That's okay, just drag your butt out of bed. Maybe you could only manage to make your kids some instant oatmeal for breakfast instead of the slow-cooked oats with fresh fruit you wanted to make. So what? At least you gave them some pretty healthy fuel so that they could go out into the world and do their best as well.

Whether it's working out or raising a family, it's okay to not be a superstar all the time. In fact, it's okay to stink it up sometimes. (Remember, failure and success are two halves of the same whole.) I'll take whatever you got, as long as it's the *best you got in that moment*. Do your best *and forget the rest*.

### WATCH YOUR FORM

Of course, there's a caveat here. When it comes to consistency, it's okay to have a subpar workout on occasion—but good form is essential at all times. Sometimes your stamina is going to be low or your agility might be off or your balance is nowhere to be found. When that happens, just take your time and be careful. If it can't happen, do something else. Worried that you'll injure your shoulder doing an upper-body workout today? Go for a run. Just get that blood and breath moving.

The same principle applies to your diet. If you're in the middle of nowhere and don't have access to the best, freshest foods, it doesn't mean you have to eat Cheetos and drink Coke. I can't tell you the number of times I've been starving at a gas station and had to settle for a bag of mixed nuts and a tall water. It's not the greatest, but it holds me over until I can have a healthy meal.

Watching your form really applies to just about everything in life—particularly when it comes to relationships. If you're running on empty, it greatly increases the chances that you'll say or do something you'll regret. So remember the basics of being a good human and say things in your head a few times before saying them out loud, or put that hastily written email in the draft folder for a couple hours before sending. Sometimes a consistent achiever is also a silent achiever.

## CONSISTENCY IN THE KITCHEN

When it comes to your diet, the most consistent factor should be quality. Keep the fruits and vegetables, whole grains, and lean proteins coming. Every meal, all the time, should support your goals and your overall lifestyle. The less you cheat, the less you suffer. Just because you ate a healthy breakfast doesn't entitle you to a fast food lunch. Ate a healthy lunch? That doesn't mean Fluffernutters on white bread with a side of Fritos for dinner.

The food you eat directly affects how much energy you'll have for your workouts. For example, B complex vitamins directly affect your metabolism. You can't properly turn food—or body fat, for that matter—into energy without a healthy supply. If you skimp on them, your ability to blast workouts suffers. Electrolytes such as potassium and magnesium influence your fluid balance. Without them, you increase your chance of cramping during intense workouts. Antioxidants like vitamins A, C, and E and zinc help to repair the breakdown (or oxidation) our body experiences during rigorous exercise, not to mention during the general stresses of life. Without them, your body lurches out of balance and you become more susceptible to disease.

At the same time, life's too short to live on steamed kale. I'm not asking you to turn into a dietary Dalai Lama. Add a little variety and try something else. My diet has consisted primarily of fresh fruits and veggies for years now and I'm still amazed when I go to the farmers' market at all the produce I haven't yet tried.

Balance is also important. Sometimes food needs to feed the spirit and only the spirit, if you catch my drift. Every now and then, it's okay to eat a little somethin'-somethin' that satisfies your sweet or savory cravings. Keep this between you, me, and the lamppost, but sometimes I'll have a couple of dark-chocolate-covered almonds or a hot chocolate chip cookie (mmm . . . chocolate). Or if I'm having a big bowl of fresh berries, I might lubricate things with a spoonful of fresh whipped cream. But these indulgences are the exception to the rule. Most of the time, I serve my meals with a hearty side of consistency.

# LAW 6

## CRANK UP THE INTENSITY

*The harder I work, the luckier I get.*

—Samuel Goldwyn

The Law of Intensity was born while I was doing pull-ups with Iron Man and Sherlock Holmes.

Okay, technically, it was Robert Downey Jr. and he had yet to play either of these roles. It was in the early nineties. I was just getting started as a trainer. He was in a dark period. How dark? Let me put it this way. He could barely pull off a couple of pull-ups.

I wasn't formally training him; we were both just working out at the same gym, and we ended up at the same pull-up bar one afternoon, which is when he asked me for some advice. I considered myself to be a pull-up master, but the truth is, I wasn't making much progress, either. I never really pushed myself back then. I'd go to the gym and phone it in: eight of these, ten of those, fifteen of that other thing—and then eight or ten pull-ups, max. Could I do eleven? I didn't know. Ten was all I ever tried.

So as I was explaining to Robert Downey Jr. how he needed to push himself to get his numbers up, it hit me like a ton of bricks: I wasn't walking the talk. I was telling him, "Just fight for one more rep." But what about me? Why wasn't *I* fighting for one more rep?

So I did. And, over time, ten became eleven, eleven became twenty, twenty became thirty. Today, in my fifties, I can do forty pull-ups in a row. Adding intensity to my workouts has helped me build the strength I need to be able to keep working out hard at my age.

Nelson Mandela once said, "There is no passion to be found in playing small—in settling for a life that is less than the one you are capable of living." Somehow, I don't think he was talking about pull-ups, but he may as well have been. For many of us, intensity starts with exercise. It empowers us to see what we're capable of in a very tangible, visceral way. I can't tell you how many times I've seen the fire ignite in people's eyes the moment they do their first real pull-up. But intensity should be about more than improving physically. It's also about digging deeper mentally and emotionally. And when you go big like that, people notice—and then they're inspired to go big, too.

Back to Iron Man for a moment. How do you think Robert Downey Jr. got his career back on track? Intensity mixed with Consistency. He worked his butt off. He ditched the bad habits, found a good support group, and pushed himself hard. Without that level of fierceness and intensity, in all likelihood, he'd still be struggling in every aspect of his life—not just pull-ups.

## INTENSITY ISN'T ALWAYS AWESOME: "THE F-16 STORY"

Sometimes intensity is completely awful—and that's a good thing. What do you learn from awesome? That life can be fun! That's about it. But awful is where all the best learning comes in. You learn the outer edge of your capabilities, as well as your limits.

I learned this lesson firsthand while hurling toward the ground in a jet fighter at Mach-something while heaving into a spent vomit bag. It was the epitome of awful and one of the great learning experiences of my life. It's one of my favorite stories to share, so get comfortable.

As the son of a father who was in the service and as a guy who is impressed by heroes of any ilk, I'm a big believer in supporting our troops and I do military tours with the Department of Defense and Armed Forces Entertainment whenever I can. So when I was invited on a nine-base tour of Japan a few years back, I jumped at the chance.

It started at Kadena Air Base in Okinawa. They call Okinawa "the Garden Island of Japan," but when I got there, it was forty-eight degrees and raining sideways. This, combined with jet lag and the fact that someone forgot to include "sleep" in our itinerary, meant that before the end of the first day I caught a brutal cold, which was a real bummer, considering that I was scheduled to fly in an F-16 on day two. But blocked sinuses be damned! I wasn't going to miss an opportunity like that, so I dragged my sleep-deprived, congested head to the six hours of preflight procedures, where I learned how to use the oxygen mask, the ejection seat and parachute, the compression suit, and all the other doo-dads I needed to understand in order to make sure I returned to the ground as a living, breathing human being.

During the training, I got to know the pilots. These guys were the real deal—it was like *Top Gun* all over again. I'd be riding with Adam "Axe" Gaudinski, who got his nickname because he flies like a hatchet, meaning he banks sharp and hard. In retrospect, I should have taken his name as an omen. Perhaps I could have asked if there were any pilots named "Feather" or, maybe, "Snail." Alas, I was flying with Axe.

Here's a little secret about me: I have kind of a weak stomach. When I get on a boat—I don't care if it's an ocean liner or an inflatable raft in a swimming pool—I get queasy. Queasy and vomiting go hand in hand with me. I'm good at throwing up. I've thrown up hundreds of times in my life. I'm a real vomit veteran. But Axe and the other pilots didn't know that. They were P90X fans, so they assumed I was some kind of tough guy. So on the morning of my flight, I tried to sound macho when I asked, "What percentage of people throw up in this thing?"

Axe responded, "Oh, it's kind of fifty-fifty. Usually we tell people, 'If you throw up just let it go and then get back in the game, enjoy the experience.'"

Enjoy the experience. Right. Maybe someone saw the concern on my face, because one of them added, "Be careful what you eat. Probably the best thing is a banana because a banana tastes the same coming up as it does going down."

The only problem was that I'd gotten some other information suggesting I should eat a big breakfast. A few hours previously, I had filled up on two bowls of oatmeal and two egg white omelets loaded with colorful veggies. And then right before we took off I threw in a protein bar because I was hungry after all that training. No bananas were involved.

The plan was to break the speed of sound, then to pull 3 g's and then 5 g's, working up to 9 g's a couple of times. (To give you some perspective, the world's fastest roller coaster, the Formula Rossa at Ferrari World in Abu Dhabi, maxes out at 1.7 g's.) After the 9 g's, they were going to let me fly the plane.

When we got out there, it was pouring rain, but we still went through the whole rigmarole. A three-star general, Lieutenant General Commander Burt Field, of the Fifth Air Force, was there with other big shots and their families, as well as my friends Mark, Robert, and Nicole, along with my girlfriend, Shawna. About fifteen or twenty people saw us off.

This was an F-16. It flies twice the speed of sound. Apparently, F-22s and F-35s are even faster, but this was certainly all the jet I needed. We broke the sound barrier and I didn't even notice until I looked at the speedometer doing 840 mph. (The boom happens behind you, so you don't get to hear it.) And then Axe says, "We're going to do our first 3g move. Here we go."

Wham! It felt like an elephant sitting on my lap. It was like being bent in half. When we came out of that, I didn't feel great. Down by my right leg, there were five plastic vomit bags. I made sure they were still there.

Next, Axe says, "All right, we're going to do 5 g's now." Bang! Up came the bar, the oatmeal, the eggs, the whole panoply of smells and colors.

Vomiting in a speeding F-16 isn't easy. I was wearing an oxygen mask, and it was pressing down on every millimeter of my flesh because you don't want cockpit air to get in there; it's bad news. You can barely gasp it. So I had to pull off the mask using this little metal latch, throw up, tie off the bag, and put it somewhere so it didn't hit me in the face later. Then I had to get the oxygen mask's latch back into the slot in order to get a proper seal on my face, which was pretty tricky, but I got it done.

At this point, the pilots decided to impress me by flying toward each other at faster than the speed of sound, but I wasn't impressed at all because my face was in my lap. The only thing I could see was this black-edged tunnel that I'm pretty sure didn't lead anywhere pleasant. You know those old movies where you'd see somebody get shot in the stomach with a cannonball? It was like that. And when I did finally look up, it was only to get my mask off again so I could puke a second time.

By the time we'd done 8.8 g's, I'd filled three vomit bags. Axe says, "It's your turn. Show me what you can do."

Here's another secret about me: I have never played a video game in my life. I wouldn't know a Wii remote from a digital thermometer. So as I grabbed the joystick, I had no idea how this multi-ton F-16 was going to react.

Axe says, "Do whatever you want, we're high enough that it doesn't really matter." So I just pulled on the joystick. Suddenly I wasn't in a jet anymore, I was in a rocket ship going straight into outer space. Someday, when I'm done here on Earth, that's generally the direction I hope to head, but I wasn't quite ready for the Pearly Gates at that moment, so I let go of the joystick (causing the plane to level out), took off the oxygen mask, and threw up again.

But Axe wasn't done with me: "Try something else. Try forward this time."

Of all the throw-up sessions, that was the worst. Suddenly I was in a bullet going straight to hell. It felt like my stomach was being shoved into my throat. It was the most excruciating feeling I've ever had. It was like having pneumonia on Mount Everest naked in a tornado.

I had run out of bags, so I started untying old ones to reuse. I have no idea what I was throwing up at that point, but it went beyond the morning's breakfast. And the thing about a jet is you're moving and banking at such high rates of speed that your whole system gets tweaked, so I was farting up a storm, too. Farting and vomiting and farting because everything was getting pushed and shoved and crushed.

Axe kept saying, "You can still fly it if you want; try something more subtle." So I turned the joystick maybe a quarter inch to the right. Now we were flying sideways. "Go a little bit more." So I did and the jet rolled.

Out the window, it was sky, ground, sky, ground. I was spinning in a tin can, which launched me into my sixth or seventh vomit fest. I was dying. It was like being run over by a train in super–slow motion.

Then Axe said, "Hey, we only got to 8.8 g's the first two times and we've got enough fuel for one more 9-g try. How do you feel?" I said, "If we attempt 9 g's, you will certainly kill me. We'll show up at the base and there'll be a corpse in the back of this jet."

I was so done. When we landed, it was the same twenty people—the same twenty happy, smiley, applauding, "Yay! Look! You did it!" people—and then I took my mask off. You could hear a gasp from the crowd. Shawna said, "Oh my God, what happened to his face?"

My skin was gray-white and just hanging from my face. I looked like an elderly shar-pei. Ever the wiseacre, Mark turned to Shawna and said, "Now you know what he's going to look like when he's eighty-five."

We got back to base and that was pretty much the end of me. I was supposed to get cleaned up and go to the PX for a book signing and then attend a fancy ceremonial dinner, but I just couldn't do it. I don't even remember falling asleep that night. I was out cold for twelve hours straight.

So what's the lesson here? First and foremost, it's crucial that you remember never, ever to eat a protein bar right before you attempt to pull 9 g's. Second, sometimes going out on a limb and doing things with intensity doesn't work out the way you might expect. I was expecting awesome, but I got awful—an awful lot of vomit, to be exact—and that's okay. When you live your life with intensity, every once in a while you'll find yourself in a vulnerable, overwhelming situation over which you have no control. This is where you have the most to learn.

That tired old cliché about getting back on the horse when you fall off is ultimate wisdom, as far as I'm concerned. I've had an offer to go up in a jet again. For the first six months after Japan, there would have been no way, but now I think I will, only this time I'll ask the pilot stay at 3 g's.

And I'm having a banana for breakfast.

## INTENSITY FOR THE REST OF US

It's easy to illustrate the Law of Intensity through stories about pull-ups and fighter jets. But the truth is, intensity applies to everything we do in subtler ways. Adding intensity to fitness is easy because it's measurable—it's just a question of adding a rep or lifting a few more pounds. In the rest of your life, it's a little trickier. This is where Law 1 comes in handy yet again: When you add intensity to doing your best and forgetting the rest, you're constantly checking in with yourself to be honest about what your best is. Maybe you're really good at trimming the hedges in the shape of penguins. When you first started doing it, your neighbors thought it was great. People drove miles to see your penguin hedges. Ten years ago, they were the best you could do. You deserved to be proud.

But guess what? That was a decade ago. Are you seriously telling me that you haven't learned to sculpt other lawn animals? Camels? Mongooses? Platypuses? Come on! It's your best only if you continue to progress. And you progress only by adding intensity. To get better, you have to focus on how you're doing things, and then make sure that your style, technique, and method are all evolving. You have to push yourself. If you're doing anything halfway you're going to get a half-baked result.

Talent and intensity are two different things. You can be an incredibly talented writer, or athlete, or shrub trimmer, but if you don't challenge yourself, you're still going to live a C-minus life.

## WHAT WE CAN LEARN FROM OUR HAMSTRINGS

If you want a perfect example of subtle intensity, look no farther than your hamstrings. A select few folks are genetically set up to be flexible behind their legs, but most of us have steel cables back there. And if you don't train and stretch them, they just get worse, eventually becoming the bane of your existence in terms of athleticism, functional movement, and quality of life. Hence the term "hamstrung"—which generally refers to being limited in your potential to achieve a desired goal.

When I'm training groups, particularly those new to exercise, I always focus on the hamstrings. I'll have everyone do a basic forward hamstring stretch (see page 179). But instead of just having them stare at their feet and mutter in pain for half a minute, I give them a little plan that dials up intensity.

Some people can barely place their hands above their knee. Others are grabbing their heel. Either way, I encourage them to look two inches farther than where they're grabbing now, which should be just slightly outside their comfort zone. I explain that I'm going to count to thirty and during that time, I want them to (1) breathe and (2) believe that they're going to extend those two inches.

If I were a sadist, I'd enjoy those next thirty seconds, watching all the grimacing, grunting, and shaking. Instead, I remind them to relax the breath, face, and mind. I assure them that they have this little plan in place and that should be their focus.

Sure enough, when we're through, I always ask for a show of hands and about 80-plus percent of the group feel they were able to increase and deepen their stretch.

Intensity is a game of mind over matter. It is always in you to do something a little better than you did it the last time. The next time you're struggling to dial up the intensity, try setting a time limit for yourself like I do with the hamstring stretch—and that advice doesn't just apply to the physical stuff. You can stretch yourself mentally or emotionally, too. Here's one of my favorites: Try to stop complaining for a whole day. No muttering about the traffic, the weather, your spouse, the newscaster's weird hair, nothing for an entire twenty-four hours. (It's hard. Trust me.)

Whatever it is, just stretch it a little, tiny bit further. Odds are, it will help you reach that much closer to your goals.

## NINE DOESN'T MEAN TEN

Intensity is tricky because it adds an element of danger to whatever you're doing (especially in a fighter jet). The key is to learn from that danger and make adjustments accordingly. It's important to be conscious of intensity. Yes, I'm going to run ten miles instead of eight. No, I'm not going to try to run it in the same amount of time as eight. Use Intensity, one of the Big Three laws for ultimate success (along with Variety and Consistency), but learn how to regulate it so that you're pushing yourself forward without hamstringing your success.

For a positive change to occur, there first needs to be a stimulus. In the world of fitness, this stimulus comes in the form of an overload. This means that you're putting greater than normal stress on the body, so the body is forced to adapt. When you combine this with the gradualism I mentioned earlier, you get gradual progressive overload. As you train over time, the overload should be slowly increased. The key to getting intensity right is knowing how to create that overload without feeling like it's miserable, without feeling like exercise is so hard that you never want to do it again. Also, too much overload too quickly can result in injury.

I see people push too hard all the time. They might take a level-one Hatha yoga class, love it, and decide to try hot yoga the next week. They end up sweaty, injured, and swearing never, ever to do yoga again.

Gradual progressive overload works outside the gym, too. Whatever you're doing, do it a little harder, but don't destroy yourself. If it takes a couple of days for you to do the *Times* crossword, try getting it done in one day. Have a dinner party for eleven instead of your usual ten. (Surely you know some bachelor in need of a home-cooked meal.)

But don't cook for thirty, or you may buckle under the pressure and never want to set foot in the kitchen again (you may also injure yourself with all of that knife work). Push your limits, but don't shove them too hard. If you go beyond your ability you'll be miserable—and you'll run out of silverware. The key is that most of us underestimate our ability, our stamina, our skill, our grit—so don't shortchange yourself. You're tougher than you think. Dial it up a notch.

## THE FOUR CLAUSES FOR SETTING YOUR INTENSITY LEVEL

Intensity is a tricky balance. You need to learn to walk the line, Johnny Cash–style. Here are four clauses of the Law of Intensity that'll help you do that:

Clause 1: Find the line. The "line" is that special place you need to get to if you want something to work. It's discovering your discomfort threshold so you can get the job done without the wheels coming off the bus. If you plain old "give up" because you "can't" do something the first few times, then you'll never know what it's like to succeed. As a general guideline, you'll find the line when you push yourself as hard as you can and still do it right (maintain proper form).

Clause 2: Understand what it means to go over and under the line. Going *under* the line means you're just dialing it in without making progress, even if it's technically a "good job." It's your own, personal lawn penguin. It's what happens when you never ask, "What about eleven?" Going *over* the line means you're consistently crashing and burning. In fitness terms, it's when you're so sore for the next three days after a workout that you can't walk, sit down, or feed yourself, let alone hit the gym again.

Clause 3: Accept that sometimes we all go over the line. Sometimes you're going to take it too far, whether you like it or not, because of circumstances that are somewhat out of your control (see F-16 story).

Don't seek out this kind of circumstance, but when it happens, accept it and realize it's an opportunity for growth, as miserable as you may be.

Clause 4: Put on the brakes. When looking for the line, you sometimes discover you've already gone over it. Luckily, you can often salvage these situations by following your intuition and using a few tricks.

Subclause a: Just stop. When you're feeling overwhelmed, it might feel counterintuitive to stop taking action. Stop anyway. Thinking on the fly is a great tool, but most of us do much better when we pause and reassess. The damage caused by temporary inaction is usually less severe than damage caused by the wrong action.

Subclause b: Proceed with caution. Far too often I see people trying to be superheroes when tackling a project. Don't do this unless you're LeBron James or Peyton Manning. Take it slow and keep thinking as you proceed. Be ready to exercise "subclause a" as needed.

Subclause c: Be done when you're done. It didn't work out this time? That's okay. It's important to recognize when it's time to stop. That's not failure. That's just being smart. As long as you live to tell the tale, you can try again, using the knowledge you gained during your first try.

### INTENSITY IN THE KITCHEN

Don't worry. I'm not going to ask you to eat with intensity. That would be weird, and besides, that's Cookie Monster's job. What I am going to suggest, however, is that you use this law to add focus to some of the other laws. Have you ever attended a holiday meal with the foregone conclusion that you were going to eat yourself sick? Have you ever flown to sunny St. Somewhere with the knowledge that you'd be seeing the sights through a coconut-rum-spiked haze? Have you ever let your grumbling tummy allow you to succumb to the call of the candy aisle at the gas station?

Making good choices in any of these situations is a first-class challenge. But I'm here to remind you: You're tougher than you think, especially if you walk into situations with an intense awareness of how important your health, your goals, your Plan, and your Purpose are.

As always, intensity goes hand in hand with consistency and variety. The combination of the three creates a platform for success. Consistency means you commit to eating what you need to succeed at each meal. Variety allows you to shift your diet when those needs change. Intensity is your lucky rabbit's foot for success. When you're in a jam, it allows you to use consistency as a beacon and variety as a tool to adapt quickly.

Think outside the cereal box. Ask yourself, "How do I eat healthy foods in tricky situations?" Sometimes the answer is obvious. At those holiday dinners, show up with some healthy food in your belly, which will help you choose wisely. That succotash might not be perfect, but it's better for you than the candied yams. Ask for turkey breast instead of thigh. Walk away from the dinner roll bowl. Use your intensity to keep the Big Picture in view. First, think about a future twenty minutes from now when you're sitting on the couch, pants unbuttoned, feeling bloated and sick. Then look at an alternative future twenty years from now, when you've followed your Plan and you're living your Purpose because you spent a lifetime making the right decisions.

# DO SCARY THINGS THAT WON'T KILL YOU

Intensity—like every one of my laws—goes beyond pushing your workouts. One of my favorite thinkers, Joseph Campbell, once wrote, "The cave you fear to enter holds the treasure you seek." To me, that means "Do scary things that won't kill you." It means you need to give life your all and take chances, or else you'll never know what you could have accomplished. In other words, intensity goes beyond exercise. Intensity is a necessary part of living your Purpose, and getting to your Big Picture.

In my opinion, the ultimate metaphor for this philosophy is my favorite way to do my favorite sport: heli-skiing.

I skied for years before I learned what heli-skiing was. I just thought that you jumped out of a helicopter and that every ride was like a scene from *Full Metal Jacket*, and every run was a dance with avalanches. But that's not the case. Could an avalanche happen? Sure. But you could also fall off the chairlift. Is that going to keep you off the mountain? I hope not.

And for the record, you don't jump out of the helicopter, unless you're shooting a Warren Miller movie. It lands, you step out, it takes off, and then you put your skis on and go skiing. Heli-skiing sounds super-crazy dangerous, but if you have the right equipment, skill, and experience, you can push past fear and be richly rewarded. Because all you're doing is turning up the volume of the experience of skiing—just like intensity turns up the volume of life.

There are a couple of things that most experienced skiers like. We like to ski steeper slopes, because that means more challenge, exhilaration, and intensity. It also means more skill and focus.

And we like our narrow runs. A big, wide, groomed slope requires less skill.

Now take those two elements and add trees, another element of intensity. So when you have a steep, narrow gulch with trees, you've got yourself one of the most technically difficult, hair-raising types of runs out there. "So," you're asking, "is that what heli-skiing is like?"

You can also add cliff bands, rocks, and tree stumps—each one amping the intensity. And then consider that a run like this, when it's easily accessible, gets chewed up pretty quickly. After a big snowstorm, everybody wants in, and everybody wants first dibs, so if you get in there late in the game, forget about it. It's shredded by ten thirty.

But not when you're heli-skiing. If you're dealing with a first-rate heli-ski operation, on every run you get fresh, untracked snow, which is every skier's dream.

Some of the runs that I've done in Blue River, British Columbia, have been the most exhilarating, exciting, incredible moments of my life. On a really good day, you can't see your skis, your feet, your knees, or anything below your chest. Snow is hitting you in the face and flying over your head. It's like floating in a cloud. You're flying without wings in a blanket of white. Sometimes you're launching off five-, ten-, fifteen-, twenty-foot cliffs and you just keep going, boom, boom, boom. I've done a lot of fun things in my life but nothing matches it in terms of pure joy. I don't know what heaven is like, but I don't know how it can be better than that.

Not only is it an intense experience, but it also requires intense training to really enjoy it. You've got to do more than just get off the couch—you've got to put in the time to enjoy the adventure. You want to experience life? Your couch days are few and far between!

There are scores of similar experiences out there in the world, but you'll never find them unless you dial up your intensity. Some of them will feel like heli-skiing in fresh powder. Some of them will feel like barfing in an F-16. All of them will be memorable. You'll learn—and live—with gusto. We all encounter daily fear in our lives, and we all have the opportunity to use intensity to conquer those fears, no matter how large or small. Intensity builds confidence. It builds ability. It heightens your desire for adventure. It heightens your level of focus. It heightens your ability to see the Big Picture.

## A FINAL NOTE ON VARIETY, CONSISTENCY, INTENSITY, AND THE BIG PICTURE

Why do you do what you do? Maybe you want to be better at a sport or a hobby. Maybe you want to be president of your company—or of your country. Maybe you want to be healthy to spend a lifetime with your kids. Maybe you just want to be generally fantastic.

That's what the Big Three are here to help you achieve. Whatever you want to do, mix it up with variety. That way you'll gather more information and improve in a variety of ways, accelerating your overall success and preventing boredom and plateaus, and in the case of physical activities, injury. Next, keep it up with consistency. After all, practice doesn't necessarily make you perfect but practice makes you better. Variety and consistency feed off each other, benefiting you exponentially. Finally, dial it up with intensity, the rocket ship to launch the benefits of variety and consistency into the stratosphere, taking you to the next level.

Doing scary things that don't kill you and working hard to get better are also going to give you lots of opportunities to spend time with family and friends—including new friends who want to do the same cool, scary things you want to do.

Now you've added yourself into the circle. A lot of these people who you're doing interesting things with have been at it for two, five, six, ten, twenty years. Their knowledge, experience, and wisdom are yours for the asking. So now you're gaining knowledge, experience, and wisdom.

Soon, you've been doing it for two, five, six, ten, twenty years yourself. You're one of those people. You're the guy or gal who heli-skis, or big-wave surfs, or competes in triathlons. You're the man or woman who calls the shots in your company. You're the god or goddess whose charity work has made a difference in other people's lives. You're the father or mother who's done an amazing job at raising your kid. And people come up to you and say, "You think you could help me do that?" And you tell them what I tell them: "Heck, man, if I can do it, you can do it. Here's how."

Leading by example, you show them that life is not about feeding your ego. Life is about living. When you know this, you become the ultimate motivator. It's not just about surviving anymore. It's about thriving and showing the people in your life how to thrive. Get out there, have a blast, and help friends, family members, co-workers, and your community to make the most of their lives.

That, in a nutshell, is the Big Picture.

# LOVE IT OR LEAVE IT

*Follow your bliss and the universe will open doors for you where there were only walls.*

—JOSEPH CAMPBELL

I t's pretty obvious by now that one of the things I love is skiing. I love the speed. I love being outside and breathing the clean air. I love how present I am when I'm out there. I love using my physical and mental skills to navigate my way to the bottom of a mountain.

In any given place and on any given day, no two runs are the same. You've got hundreds of choices, and hundreds of changes. Snow, light, temperature, humidity, and snow density all shift across the day, so each run will be different from the morning to midday to the afternoon. If anyone understands the law of variety, it's Mother Nature.

I don't love traditional workouts. For me, a biceps curl isn't as fun (or as cool) as making my way around a pegboard. Bench pressing isn't as much fun as four ball push-ups. And lat pulls? Why do that when I can climb a rope? I'm having a blast doing skill exercises, and I'm dealing with hand strength, gravity, and a touch of fear. I'm getting a physical, mental, and emotional challenge. In other words, I'm loving it.

## WHY DO WE NEED TO LOVE IT?

Are you seriously asking why you need to love it? It's not like I'm asking you to eat your brussels sprouts (although you should do that, too). Well, I can give you three reasons "why." The short answer is that loving it means you're *having fun*, and it's essential to keep fun in the mix as you execute the Plan that will lead you to your goals. All work and no play makes Tony a dull boy—and my guess is, it also makes you a lot less motivated to be consistent and stick to your Plan.

The slightly longer answer is that life is too short not to explore things you love. And, quite frankly, if you're not getting any enjoyment out of a particular activity or a particular part of your life, I would question whether that activity (or habit or person) is really in line with your Purpose (more on that later).

The much longer answer requires a little science to explain fully. Excuse me while I change into my lab coat . . .

Our bodies—yours, mine, your kids', your parents'—are regulated by chemicals called hormones. There are hundreds of different kinds of hormones in the body, each with its own specific functions; there are hormones that regulate hunger; hormones that affect sex drive; hormones that influence mood—there's not much that happens in our bodies that hormones don't affect in some way.

They do this by acting as chemical messengers. For instance, when the body wants fuel, the stomach and pancreas secrete a hormone called ghrelin, which travels to the brain and tell us it's time for lunch (preferably a healthy one). Then, once we've had enough to eat, the hormone leptin, which mainly comes from our fatty tissue, is released to tell us we're full. Our hormones are affected by our food choices, sleeping habits, health, environments, physical activity, stress level, and a number of other things. In a nutshell: Our hormones regulate us, but we can also regulate them right back.

Adrenaline, as you've probably heard, is one of your "fight or flight" hormones. Your adrenal glands pumps out adrenaline in response to immediate stress, sending a panic button message to multiple areas of your body: It elevates your heart rate and your blood pressure, dilates air passages and blood vessels, speeds up metabolism, and sharpens your senses. This served us well back in the day if we had to sprint from a saber-toothed tiger during a hunting trip gone wild, and it serves me well today when I'm making split-second decisions and movements as I barrel down the side of a mountain at 55 mph.

But adrenaline is to your body what nitrous tanks are to a drag racer. It gives your engine a big boost, but if you stay elevated for too long, you're going to burn out. So your adrenal glands follow up adrenaline with another hormone called norephedrine, which basically brings your operating systems back to normal. It slows everything down, including brain function and metabolism.

It makes sense that your body gives you the advantage of being faster, stronger, and more powerful when you're under *acute* stress and you need to stay alive. In stressful conditions, cortisol raises your blood pressure, elevates blood sugar, and diverts energy from other tasks to whatever is mission critical. But our bodies aren't built for sustained periods of *chronic* stress, which is how many of us live today. We are well equipped to sprint from that tiger, but we're just not built to endure year upon year of working a sixty- to eighty-hour-a-week in a job we don't particularly like.

Continued cortisol release takes a toll after a while. To keep blood pressure up, cortisol retains sodium (and water) in your cells. To keep blood sugar up, it breaks down muscle into glucose. And in diverting energy, it inhibits other bodily functions that may not be as immediately important—such as digestion. The whole process also burns through vitamins and minerals like crazy. And here's the real kicker. Visceral fat—the kind that gathers around your gut, commonly associated with type 2 diabetes and cardio-vascular issues—is a particularly good cortisol source, so when you're under prolonged stress, you divert fat from other parts of your body to your belly—your big, stressed-out beer belly. An overabundance of cortisol can also lead to illnesses like chronic fatigue syndrome and depression.

There are lots of supplements out there that are supposed to mitigate the effects of cortisol, but in my opinion, *the best way to get rid of a problem is to get rid of the problem*. In other words, the best way to get rid of an illness is to stop feeding it.

The best way to get rid of cortisol is to learn how to control your stress.

And the best way to stop stressing is to love what you're doing: to *have some fun*. If you live in a chronic state of stress and anxiety, it's inevitable that depression, fatigue, and a few extra pounds will be your constant companions. Having fun is not only a crucial component of reaching your Big Picture goals; it's also good for your health. And when you're healthy, you're better able to get out there and have fun and be productive. See how the cycle works? Law 7 may seem more trivial than the others at first—but look at the rogue's list of the twenty-first century's most common maladies I just listed. Having fun—loving it—isn't just crucial so that you can thrive. It's crucial so that you can *survive*.

What's more, when you really think about it, Loving It is what life is all about. Without that you have no Purpose, no Plan, no consistency/intensity/variety. You're just going through the motions.

I'm not asking you to walk away from all your unpleasant tasks in favor of a life filled with mindless hedonism (although that sounds tempting). What I'm asking is that you make a point of prioritizing fun in your life, the same way you prioritize all your other important tasks. Who knows—your life could depend on loving it.

## LOVING IT EVERYWHERE

**IF YOU'RE A PARENT, THIS IS CALLED HAVING "MOM TIME" OR "DAD TIME."** For example, if you really love *Monday Night Football*, take a stand that once a week, the world stops while you get your game on. Those couple of hours will let you be a more attentive, less resentful parent the rest of the time.

**AT HOME, KEEP IN MIND THAT IT'S YOUR HOME.** You call the shots (to some degree). If you're a little slow at folding the laundry or raking the yard because you spent an extra hour sledding with your kids (not on Monday night, of course), it's no big deal.

And keep in mind that there's a difference between loving it and being distracted. For example, television. Do you really love the boob tube that much? If so, well, I guess that's great, but if you're like most people, it's just a distraction much of the time—and you shouldn't be distracted from having fun—so make a point of turning it off every so often.

IN THE WORKPLACE . . . I know this one can be tricky. We live in a workaday world. I get it. In the long term, though, I can categorically say that if you don't love your job—or at least like it—you should have a Plan in place to change that. In the short term, at the very least, go out to lunch with your favorite workmates a few times each week. No one—and I mean no one—should chain themselves to the desk at lunch hour with a nuked Cup o' Noodles.

## AVOIDING THE BOREDOM TIPPING POINT (BPT)

What does it mean to love it, or at least enjoy it? I think about it from an exercise perspective (surprised?): When people find a fitness program they love, they're excited to do it. Having a routine (consistency) is essential when someone's getting into a program—it helps you to form good habits and makes you commit to the program—but routine is also what causes folks to quit after a while. Just because you love something at the outset doesn't mean you're going to love it forever.

When it comes to your day-to-day activities, the same principle applies. When you start a new job, you're excited and optimistic. Having a consistent routine keeps you disciplined and on top of your game. But after a while, that regularity can be boring. When the bright, shiny, and new wear off, you can fall into the routine of clocking in, getting through the day, clocking out, and counting down to the weekend. And being on autopilot at work (or in any part of life) is rarely a good thing.

When you've gotten to that point, you've already crossed the threshold of what I call the boredom tipping point, or the BTP.

The boredom tipping point is that exact moment when an activity becomes stale. It's the moment you recognize that you're no longer engaged or motivated by the plug-and-play thing you're doing—and it's time for a change. The best way to avoid getting derailed, stuck, or quitting something altogether is to be on the lookout for the BTP and identify it as soon as it sets in.

People think boredom is just a temporary state that they need to push through, but I disagree. I think boredom is your body's and mind's way of telling you that it's time to wake up and rethink your strategy. When it comes to exercise, the evidence shows that this lack of awareness often ends up causing injury on top of the boredom. Think about it—you've been running the same five miles every day for a year. As you get bored, you're not into it, you don't stretch as much before you run, you pay less attention to how your feet are landing on the ground, to the environment around you. And then one day—whammo—you roll your ankle or blow out your knee. Because you were too bored to be engaged with what you were doing.

Relationships are especially vulnerable to boredom. I'm not telling you to get a new partner every time things start to feel stale. On the contrary—if you're vigilant and you keep an eye on your relationship, the *moment* you hit the BTP, you'll know it's time to spice things up. Avoiding it or hoping it will improve is not the answer. A relationship in a small downswing is much easier to repair than one where two people wake up one day and realize they've been bored for fifteen years.

When you hit the BPT in any part of your life, it's time to dump your current routine and find a way to love it again. I consciously make efforts to avoid boredom by trying new things, changing up my activities, and surrounding myself with people who challenge me. It keeps me on my toes, it keeps me curious and creative—and it keeps the fun factor high.

My favorite way to keep my relationship fresh is the Random Act of Variety. Whether you're planning a picnic, filling the house with roses, sending him or her a mushy postcard when you're on a business trip, or agreeing to watch that Jane Austen movie she wants to see (Ladies, please replace "Jane Austen" with "Tom Clancy" for that last one), if you want a good relationship, both parties have to go out of their way and do nice things for the other person in spontaneous and unexpected ways. Love is more than assuming that this is your roommate who will cook meals for you while you pay the bills. A lasting relationship takes work. It should be fun work, but it is work.

You also need to make sure you're on the same page in the bedroom. (Can you believe you're about to get bedroom advice from Tony the trainer?) You need to communicate about your wants and needs. Both parties have to be willing to play the same game. If you have a complaint about what happens behind closed doors and you're more willing to bring it up with your friends than your partner, that's a red flag. So take a deep breath and tell him or her what's up—or write it down if you need to. Don't let embarrassment get in the way of creating the best life you can have with each other. After all, what's a little blushing between lovers?

## OUTING YOUR INNER CHILD

I'm amazed at the number of people who don't have a hobby. They have nothing outside of family, finances, work, or fitness. They have nothing that they're really excited about—the way I'm excited about skiing. When we were kids, these kinds of activities weren't called hobbies. They were just really cool things that you did because you didn't have a job (other than making your bed and doing your homework). Everything was a hobby. You did soapbox derby, rode bikes with your friends, and played hide-and-seek. These were things you got excited about. There were lessons to be learned so that you could grow up to be a good adult, but everything else you did was just for the fun of it.

The only problem is that many of us adults have taken our roles as mature human beings to an extreme. Life becomes all about work, responsibilities, obligations, and survival. No more fun for you! When you're not actively tapping into that joyful part of yourself, you're not feeding the soul; you're not honoring your true self. And when you become a shell of your former self, you start to cut other corners, too—it's a slippery slope. You don't eat as well as you should, you don't exercise regularly, you don't spend enough time with friends and family. Eventually, your spectrum of fun things to do disappears.

You need to play again. Take some of the attention off dead-lines, stress, and corporate promotions. Take the attention off weight, inches, and body fat percentages and put the focus on having more *fun*. I don't care if it's ballroom dancing, rock climbing, mountain biking, or Ping Pong. Can't think of any-thing? Ask your friends what they do for fun. (I can teach you my dance moves, if you want. My robot is second to none.) At the start, it doesn't even have to be that physical. Maybe it's journaling, scrapbooking, coin collecting, or playing the gui-tar. I love incorporating a little physical activity into my hob-bies. Get moving with an eye toward lifting your fitness level so that you can take on more *active* activities. ("Active activities" sounds redundant, but it's not. My editor promised.) You don't need to give up playing the guitar; just turn it into one of many hobbies.

I can't tell you how many people I've met who were overwhelmed, out of shape, and unhappy but managed to turn their lives around by incorporating a little playtime here and there so that, today, they sign up for every 5K and 10K race they can find within a fifty-mile radius of their house. They do mud runs, color runs, and warrior dashes. Have you ever tried one? They're fun and filled with people just like you. So come on, it's time to tell your inner child to go out and play.

## FIND YOUR CIRCLE OF FRIENDS

Becoming an active participant in the outside world will also give you the opportunity to form meaningful connections with others—and that's a huge part of the Big Picture. Whether you're single or partnered with someone, being out and about gives you a chance to meet like-minded folks. The people I know who regularly participate in a sport they love are not only fit and happy; they also have a whole community of quality people to keep them company.

In fact, hanging around other adventurous people who do other interesting things is key to making your life an adventure. It's how you suck the life out of every second you have here on Earth. Take my Sunday Cirque du Soleil–wannabe workouts. That's not a routine I would do alone. I show up every Sunday morning to hang with the crew. The workout is killer, but we're really there for the camaraderie, laughter, and encouragement.

Over the years, I've lost count of how many Big Picture experiences I've had during my Sunday-morning workouts. I've met several people who were once strangers and have become close friends and who have had a huge impact on my life: Chuck Gaylord, Scott Fifer-Scissors, Rob Cowel, Sean Callahan, Rami Ghandour, and Jameson Hester, to name a few. I mention these guys by name because they're true friends. They inspire, motivate, and push me to be a better human being physically, mentally, and emotionally.

And once you've assembled your tribe, yet another fantastic thing happens: You find yourself surrounded by mentors who push you and teach you and advise you. In turn you push, teach, and advise them. When you choose to do active things with others—join a team, sign up for a competition, go to group class. It's inevitable that you'll become part of the Big Picture.

## LIFE ISN'T ALWAYS GOING TO BE A PARTY

I don't know about you, but I'm not motivated to do things I don't enjoy. This is why I don't knit. It is also why I am no longer a professional mime.

But sometimes Loving It isn't about Loving Every Second of It. Loving It can be about a means to an end—putting in the hours doing something that you don't love, for a result that you do love. When it comes to your exercise regimen, these kinds of trade-offs are essential for keeping you on track. For instance, do you really love push-ups? Do they get you to spring out of bed in the morning? Do you save up vacation time so you can spend most of it doing push-ups? Do you bore the in-laws watching hours and hours of video featuring you doing push-ups?

I'm betting you don't. I don't, either, but I understand their importance. As with all exercise, they allow me to move my blood and breath on a daily basis, which I know will help me physically, mentally, and emotionally. The same thing goes for all of the leg strengthening work I do—I would never jump off boxes and do so many plyometric moves if it weren't for the fact that I ski. Because I love skiing, I put in some time doing things I don't love so that I can reap the rewards of shredding my way down a mountain.

When you have a hobby, sport, or physical activity that you're passionate about, your fitness regimen serves your skill and ability in that arena—so you can put the daily exercise grind into perspective and actually make it more fun. You're not just surviving. You're not just thriving. You're striving to get the most out of the things you're passionate about. Your day-to-day workouts become less of a chore and more of an investment in a goal that you're excited about achieving.

This same approach can also help you weigh whether or not to do all the things in life that you don't necessarily love to do. Ask yourself, "Why am I doing this?" Even if you don't love the activity, check in to see if there's a Big Picture reason for doing it. Take, for example, my Tony Horton Couples' Therapy advice on page 108; I don't love sitting through the latest Hollywood rom-com, but I do love my relationship, so it's worth the ninety-minute investment. No one likes changing a poopy diaper, but I bet you love the little kid it's wrapped around. No one likes mowing the lawn, but it's always fun barbecuing in a well-kept yard (and you get a little cardio to boot). Paying bills is a drag, but you love your home, right? If not, the adjustment isn't to stop paying the rent or mortgage. The adjustment is to figure out how to get yourself into a place you want to live in. Or how to make some extra cash so paying bills isn't quite as painful. It might take a little time to reach the place you want to be, but if you have a Plan and keep your eye on your Purpose, you'll get there.

But the path to fulfilling your Purpose should not be one of misery. Instead, try to balance the good times and the not-so-good times. The chart on the next page should help with that. You may not Love It all the time, but if you're Loving It most of the time, that's where you want to be.

## Are You Loving It Enough?

Here's a simple way to determine if you're Loving It enough. Take seven photocopies of the chart that follows. For the next week, check in each hour to see if you're having fun. If so, circle "fun." If not, circle "not fun." Fun doesn't necessarily mean play. It could be some cool tasks you're doing at work, or a really awesome afternoon nap, or a great meal.

If you're in the middle of having fun, you don't need to stop what you're doing to log in. (The other folks on your soccer team might be a little PO'd.) Just make a mental note and fill it out when you have a free moment.

When you're done, count up all your fun hours and your not-fun hours. Do the "funs" have it? Then you're off to a good start! If not, maybe it's time to rethink things a little.

(Another neat thing about this chart is that it gives you perspective regarding the fun moments throughout your day. As we all know, not-fun hours tend to drag. Being able to look at this chart might help you note that, overall, life is more enjoyable than it seems.)

| | FUN | NOT FUN |
|---|---|---|
| 12 am | FUN | NOT FUN |
| 1 am | FUN | NOT FUN |
| 2 am | FUN | NOT FUN |
| 3 am | FUN | NOT FUN |
| 4 am | FUN | NOT FUN |
| 5 am | FUN | NOT FUN |
| 6 am | FUN | NOT FUN |
| 7 am | FUN | NOT FUN |
| 8 am | FUN | NOT FUN |
| 9 am | FUN | NOT FUN |
| 10 am | FUN | NOT FUN |
| 11 am | FUN | NOT FUN |
| 12 pm | FUN | NOT FUN |
| 1 pm | FUN | NOT FUN |
| 2 pm | FUN | NOT FUN |
| 3 pm | FUN | NOT FUN |
| 4 pm | FUN | NOT FUN |
| 5 pm | FUN | NOT FUN |
| 6 pm | FUN | NOT FUN |
| 7 pm | FUN | NOT FUN |
| 8 pm | FUN | NOT FUN |
| 9 pm | FUN | NOT FUN |
| 10 pm | FUN | NOT FUN |
| 11 pm | FUN | NOT FUN |

# LEAVING IT

There's a difference between doing something you don't want to do because it achieves a higher goal and doing something you don't want to do when there's no good reason to do it in the first place.

In other words, if you don't love it *and* it doesn't serve your purpose, then you should leave it. Life is too short to be filled with unnecessary burdens—and all the cortisol you're building up when taking on those burdens will only make it shorter. Taking on challenges is great, but if you're adding stress to your life, you had better make sure there's an endgame that's worth it. If the light at the end of your tunnel isn't filled with sunshine and double rainbows that you can reach within a reasonable, defined time frame—maybe you should get out of the tunnel.

Here's a classic example of what I'm talking about: relationship drama. Boy meets girl. Boy and girl fall in love. When the honeymoon ends, boy and girl find themselves in constant conflict. Boy and girl break up. Boy and girl get back together. Over and over. Both boy and girl bend over backward to try to make one another happy, because they think they're in love, and that enduring a little strife will be worth it in the long run.

But if boy and girl find that they're making themselves (and each other, and everyone around them) unhappy, that they're chronically stressed out because of the strain their relationship places on their lives, that the stress from their relationship is causing them to be less physically and mentally capable in other areas of their lives, what is the value in staying together? We know the effects of stress—when we're doing things that we not only don't love, but actually make us unhappy, anxious, and stressed out, we're taking a huge toll on our health. And I can't think of a single thing that justifies living in a state of stress and unhappiness indefinitely.

I'm all for the notion that "it's worth it in the long run," but not if it really isn't. There's no point in spinning your wheels in a bad relationship or a dead-end job—or in pursuit of an unattainable goal—if the payout isn't worth it.

How do you know if this is the case? Ask yourself these three questions:

1. Am I making progress? When you look in the rearview mirror, there should be a lot of landscape back there. If you're still where you were a year ago, something is very wrong.
2. Am I fulfilled? After a hard day of doing what you're doing, you should be able to hit the sack knowing you did your best and forgot the rest.
3. Am I still loving it—at least a little bit? Even if it's a tough job, it shouldn't tear you apart to the point that the rest of your life stinks.

If you answered "no" to these questions, it might be time to reevaluate what you're doing. How do you do that? I'm glad you asked! All you need to do is review chapters 2 and 3. First, figure out your Purpose. Second, formulate a Plan.

If you can't figure out a feasible Plan—or if you've already been through all this and your Plan just isn't working—I suggest you revisit your Purpose. (I did this quite a few times on the road to success.) Maybe by tweaking that Purpose slightly, you'll be able to formulate a better Plan—one that allows you to love it.

Let's say you decide your Purpose is to be a successful crime novel writer, so you set up a Plan that involves moving to a publishing mecca like New York, living cheap, working in a diner, and spending every free moment writing and submitting novels.

Five years later, you're still at it. You're broke, you're sick of living in the city, and you really haven't made any progress. Time to reevaluate. Maybe your Purpose was a little too specific, so you change it. Your new Purpose is to be a successful ~~crime novel~~ writer. Suddenly a better Plan comes into view. You land a job writing for a newspaper in a smaller town better suited to your tastes and temperament. Now you're a paid writer and it feels great. (Even though, given a typical journalist's salary, you're probably still broke, but so what? You're Loving It!) Your newfound job satisfaction gives you more happiness, energy, and enthusiasm—and what do you do with it? You keep working on your crime novels in your spare time. Your dream never died. You just shifted your life around, filling it full of fulfillment, and making the journey all the more pleasant.

My point is this: Quitting doesn't always mean "giving up." Sometimes it means having the integrity to admit that a Plan you've invested time and energy into isn't working. Having the strength to walk away means that you can begin to invest anew in something you do love. It's worth the risk.

## AGAIN WITH THE DANGER

The Law of Loving It really shines when you mix it up with the Law of Intensity. It's all about doing those scary, wonderful things that won't kill you. This intersection means exploring areas that you're not familiar with, that you're not necessarily comfortable with. It means pushing your boundaries so that you can grow physically, mentally, and emotionally.

Write down every cool thing you've ever wanted to do. Is it dancing the tango? Is it skydiving? Is it asking that handsome guy with the glasses who works at the bookstore out to dinner? (It's the twenty-first century. Go for it!) It all comes down to trying scary things that won't kill you. Whatever it is, do it. (For the record, skydiving is easy. You just need giant cojones and the willingness to sign a lot of liability disclaimers.) Do it with everything you've got. Even if you're already good at a bunch of things, do other things. Oftentimes really successful people can be freaked out by the idea of failing. Don't worry about it. Be in the moment, be present, and be okay with the fact that you're not perfect. In other words: Do your best with intensity and fun—forget being a perfectionist.

Time and time again, I've seen folks walk into my fitness classes with fear written all over their faces. They're petrified because they're doing exercises that they've never done before, in front of a room full of strangers. What if they can't make it through the class? What if they pull something? What if they topple over in the middle of a set of wacky jacks or donkey kicks?

The plain truth is that we all look a little silly doing wacky jacks. In fact, that's the point of these exercises—it's about *having fun*. I'm not telling you to do truly dangerous things if you don't feel confident about making it out alive. I wouldn't advise you to wrestle an alligator for the challenge of a new experience and the hope of a good calorie burn. But don't use excuses to keep yourself from having fun. So you have a bum knee and you're afraid to go to a Spinning class. Fine. Can you train your upper body or go for a swim? The dangers we perceive in our minds are close bedfellows with fear. And you know how I feel about fear.

This chapter is all about loving it. Loving it requires you to actually have a good time. And as far as I know, it's pretty much impossible to have a good time if you're afraid all the time.

## WHERE YOUR MOM WAS RIGHT

Sometimes people ask me where I work out. And the truth is, I have a home gym behind my house (hey, it's Los Angeles—a lot of people do). But I don't consider that space to be my only gym.

My other gym is planet Earth and all the obstacles on it. The moguls, the crags, the hills, the valleys, the trails. To me, there is nothing better than taking my indoor training into the outside world. My sports involve cool, crisp air, gorgeous views, and climbing up or ripping down mountains. When I'm skiing, rock climbing, or working out on the beach, I'm one with my surroundings. I'm happy as a clam and at peace with the universe. (I have no idea if clams are really happy, but let's just assume they are.)

Frankly, I don't care if your bliss involves a snowy slope or a patch of dirt behind your barn. Find something that gets you out into the great outdoors where you can breathe fresh air and get a little vitamin D boost. It's like what your mom, when she wasn't being overprotective, used to say: "Just go outside and play."

## ADVICE FROM THE EXPERTS

### Stephanie Saunders, Director of Fitness, Beachbody

I like to think of Stephanie Saunders as my Girl Friday of Fitness. (Were I politically correct, I'd say "Woman Friday," but that kills the joke.)

From the moment she walked into my gym a few years back to help put the finishing touches on P90X2, she's been an indispensable part of my team. As she puts it, we had "an instantaneous work connection."

Steph has twenty years of experience under her belt as a professional dancer and fitness instructor. (Apparently, she started instructing when she was three years old.) She helps me with the nitty-gritty of my programs, there in the trenches every day, watching me create moves, name moves, and come up with sequences.

Steph is a kindred spirit in that she understands the value of making moves that are multifunctional and fun. She's also the inspiration for P90X's Saunders Stretch Cycle—and I can pay a person no greater compliment than naming an exercise move after them.

Why is she in this chapter? Because she's great at helping me do what I love—create killer workouts. Here's how we do it.

**TONY:** Let's talk a little about how we create exercises.

**STEPH:** Well, as I'm guessing you know, your ideal is to make every exercise as compound as possible, meaning to engage as many muscle groups as you can. You also try to work as many energy systems as possible. And then, of course, everything has to be fun and ideally different. We try not to repeat anything, so we're constantly coming up with ways to tweak exercises to make them different.

**TONY:** Well said. That was a test. You passed.

**STEPH:** Gosh, thanks!

**TONY:** And now for extra credit, tell me a little about a typical workday in the gym.

**STEPH:** We don't waste a lot of time, generally. I show up, we go up to the gym, and we pick a workout. Usually I've outlined it in some form so we have some skeleton to go from, but you tend to scratch that completely and give me your idea instead. Then we just start bouncing ideas off one another until something sticks.

**TONY:** We do have fun, don't we?

**STEPH:** We certainly do. It's very fun. We've both said that it's the favorite part of our jobs.

**TONY:** You've worked with a lot of trainers over the years. What is different about the way we approach exercise?

**STEPH:** Many of the trainers I've worked with get stuck into the idea that "this needs to look a certain way because my nine certifications say this and my four college degrees say that." It tends to make it very narrow and that's why a lot of workouts out there look similar. You're a certified personal trainer, but you don't get stuck in the rules, so you tend to be extremely creative, to think outside the box.

**TONY:** Exactly! Let's look at the bigger picture now. What role does creativity play in fitness in your opinion?

**STEPH:** It completely depends on the branch and who is teaching it. Everything has been done; let's be realistic. A lunge is a lunge, a squat is a squat, a push-up is a push-up, and a pull-up is a pull-up. It is how we manipulate it and change it and make it more interesting. Not only does it need to change the body but it has to be entertaining and challenging.

Yes, you can spend your whole life doing squats and lunges and push-ups and pull-ups and probably get pretty decent results, but you're going to fall asleep halfway through doing it. So creativity, to me, is everything.

**TONY:** What's your favorite workout we've worked on together?

**STEPH:** Agility-X in P90X3. It's amazing how much fun a workout can be with a couple of four-foot strips of tape on the floor. You're running, jumping, leaping, and bounding with both hands and feet. It's insane and yet really, really fun.

**TONY:** That's how we roll.

**STEPH:** Indeed, we do.

# GET REAL

*Reality isn't what the world brings to you. It's what you bring to that world.*
—T. S. HORTONHEAD

There are a few constants in life. Death . . . taxes . . . Donald Trump's hair . . . and the fact that you don't need that coffee cake sitting on your counter. You know what I'm talking about—the slice that you're currently trying to justify eating. Yes, there are some things in this world that you can't change, but for the most part, you can have a huge impact on your state of being simply by confronting it.

There are two kinds of people in this world. (I'm usually not a fan of clichéd maxims, but if the cliché fits . . .) The first kind is willing to acknowledge and confront challenges. These are the folks who are honest with themselves, who are constantly checking in, and who have the self-awareness to call a spade a spade. They admit to areas that need improvement, flaws in judgment, mistakes made. And once they've identified what's broke, they go about fixing it. These people have a tendency to go far in life. I call them the Seekers.

The second kind of people often appear to be clueless about their situation in life and the world around them. Instead of facing their problems, they bury their heads in the sand and hope everything will be magically repaired. They take no accountability for errors or mistakes. They have a hard time being honest with themselves about anything. I call these people the Hiders.

The Hiders have much in common with another breed I mentioned in chapter 1, the New Haters. Both groups are afraid of change and don't like to try new things. Truth is, they could all probably figure out their problems if they weren't so scared of what they might find. They're like me when I was younger in that they fear confrontation. But like the fortune cookie says, "It's difficult to see the forest for the trees when your eyes are six inches underground." (Actually, I've never read that in a fortune cookie, but it would make a good one. Note to self: Start high-fiber, gluten-free fortune cookie company.)

As it turns out, fit and healthy people generally fall into the Seeker category. They're constantly taking stock of their lives, evaluating what they could be doing differently or better, keeping it Real. Sometimes I work with Hiders. Oftentimes they are overweight and out of shape and they insist there's nothing they can do about it. They tell me they've tried everything, and this must just be how they have to live their lives. They feel unlucky and out of control. But then I do a little digging and discover they're skipping workouts or sneaking off-limits foods. They're not putting in the time or keeping themselves accountable. External forces aren't failing them. Their internal forces are.

For Law 8 I want to focus a little more closely on the mental and emotional aspects of the Big Picture. Because (listen up, all you Hiders out there): It's time to deal with your life, recognize the hand you've had in it, and realize that there's more to *reality* than dancing stars, hoarders, and Kardashians.

## GET REAL ABOUT YOUR ATTITUDE

You have complete control over your life and you may not even realize it. I know that sounds too good to be true—after all, your life is a big, complex subject! Bills to pay, kids to chauffeur, mothers-in-law, bosses, Facebook status updates, viral kitty videos . . . and you're so busy it's been two months since you've trimmed your nose hairs or gotten a manicure. It's all too much to manage! Let's say I agree. What's the best way to understand something that's complex? You break it down into manageable pieces.

So now it's time to get real. Even though it's complex, it's not complicated. Let's understand the difference between external forces in your life, and your ability to react and respond to them—the internal forces.

External forces are the things that you are bombarded with every single day—traffic, bad weather, work, email, phone calls, illness, fatigue, family obligations, gas prices, lions, tigers, and bears—oh my! Am I getting real enough for you? All of these external forces have one thing in common: They are coming at you whether you like it or not. So how do you successfully walk the tightrope without getting knocked off? It all comes down to having a Plan. How are you going to react when the forces hit the fan? (Hopefully, by the time you're done with this book, you'll be ready for just about anything life throws at you.)

Your internal forces are your responses to the daily onslaught of external forces. They give you the strength to rise up and take control of the life-altering moments where you can determine your destiny instead of letting outside circumstances determine it for you. They don't always look like life-altering moments—they masquerade as everyday decisions. But make no mistake, these moments matter. Your internal forces are paramount. They are everything.

Let's say you decide to get off the couch Saturday morning and take up your buddy's invite to play Ultimate Frisbee. Once you get to the park, a pretty girl on the other team catches your eye, so you introduce yourself. A year later, you're happily married.

Or maybe you put your hand up to help with the food drive your company puts on every November. A couple of months later, the corporate bean counters decide it's time to tighten their belts with a round of layoffs. It's down to you and a couple of others—then they notice your volunteer record and decide they need to keep team players like you around, so your job is saved.

Good things happen, and the better you position yourself, the better your chances of having those good things happen to you.

How are you currently dealing with what life is throwing at you? Are you screaming at your kids when they get on your nerves? Do you shut down and give your spouse the silent treatment after a bad day at work? Are you crying to your friends about some perceived slight or insult that doesn't have any real impact on your life? If any of this sounds like you, then pay very close attention to this next part: These types of reactions are going to kill you (remember what stress does to your body?). Do you want to be on the Big Picture team or do you want to be part of the problem? Behavior like this is not part of the Big Picture. You, and only you, can take the steps to begin to shift your thinking.

By changing your reactions to what life offers you, you can become someone who chooses what to accept, who creates the life they want to live.

This may sound like a huge task, but it's not. It's simply a matter of learning to recognize the things that don't matter so that you can *let them go*. Does it really matter that someone cut you off in traffic? You're safe. Your car is fine. You're still going to get to your feng shui class on time. And, frankly, your middle finger isn't going to do anything to change the behavior of the offending driver. In fact, if he did it to spite you (which is highly unlikely), you probably just made his day. There's an old parable that sums up what I'm talking about here.

One day, a Seeker and a Hider were walking in the woods when they came across a rich woman who needed to cross a muddy creek, but she didn't want to ruin her fancy robes. Upon seeing them, she demanded they help her across.

The Hider recognized the opportunity to make a little money, but he didn't want to get dirty. So he said to his friend, the Seeker, "This lady's rich. Carry her across and we might score some cash!"

The Seeker wasn't concerned about a reward. However, he was a good guy, so he picked up the old woman and waded across, drenching his pants and ruining his sandals in the process. Once they were across, the woman just walked away without offering a reward—or even saying "thank you," for that matter.

The Seeker looked down at his muddy feet. Without skipping a beat, he took off his sandals, tied them together, and slung them over his shoulder in the hope that they'd be okay once they dried. With that, he continued down the path.

The two men walked a while farther. The Seeker held his head high, enjoying the sunny day and the feeling of the warm earth on his toes. The Hider, on the other hand, stared at the ground, fuming. Finally, he couldn't handle it. "Dude!" he said. "Thanks to that woman, your sandals are shot. She was awful! You should be majorly pissed off! Why aren't you mad?"

The Seeker looked at his friend, smiled, and said, "I set that woman down two miles back. Why are *you* still carrying her?"

## IT'S ALL ABOUT HOW YOU REACT

Two different people can have the same encounter but experience it *in completely different ways.* No two people will react the same way to any given situation—because no two people perceive the situation the same way. The two guys in that story are a perfect example, but it goes beyond being a Seeker or a Hider. For instance, two people doing a workout program are not going to make the exact same progress and experience the exact same physical changes. Some people have weight to gain; some have weight to lose. Some people are naturally coordinated and have balance and endurance, while others may still need to work on it.

Understanding your physical, mental, and emotional reality is the first step in making lasting, positive change. When you have a firm grasp on your individuality, desires, strengths, and weaknesses, you will be better equipped to see your reality for what it is, and take the steps required to shape your life into what you want it to be (not what you've been fooling yourself into thinking it "has" to be).

I'll tell you now, it's not going to be easy. The external forces—Hiders, New Haters, the media, the checkout guy at the grocery store who swears Zumba cured his acne, false prophets, and real jerks—are all selling you a bill of goods. Meanwhile, internal forces—your insecurities, doubts, the devil on your shoulder—are doing the same thing. It's up to you to cut through all that static. (Again, my plan is that the lessons in this book will help you do that.)

Your personal reality—the framework from which you react to any given situation—is jam-packed with variables. It's as unique as your DNA. How much stress are you under? Are you getting enough sleep? Are you eating foods that give you energy and make you feel good? Do you have a support system at home? Are you following a Plan, or are you just hoping you have the winning lotto ticket?

Because we are all coming at life from different points of view, we're all going to have different reactions to external forces. You can never truly understand someone else's personal reality. Hiders are often critical of other people's lives and decisions because they're afraid to examine their own. But Seekers can respect others' choices, because they've done enough work on themselves to know that you can never truly understand what it's like to be the person sitting next to you.

## THE WHY GAME

At some point in your life, you've participated in the Why Game. It starts with a kid—maybe your son, daughter, niece, nephew, or just some annoying punk—asking you a question. When you answer, they respond with "Why?" When you respond to that, they issue another "Why?" If you play through, the game ends when your only possible response is "Because! Now shut up!"

As it turns out, the Why Game isn't just for kids. Engineers also use it to get to the root of design issues. It was developed by Toyota, where it was named "The Five Whys" because they felt that's how many whys you need to get to the heart of a problem.

But why should kids and nerds have all the fun? The Why Game is a perfect way to explore your personal reality. Start by asking yourself a question relating to internal or external forces that trouble you. "Why don't I have a girl/boyfriend?" "Why do I fight with my coworkers?" "Why am I so tired all the time?"

Now answer that question as quickly and honestly as possible. "Because I never meet new people." "Because they annoy me." "Because I'm overworked." Then ask yourself "Why?" again.

"Because I don't get out of my house enough." "Because I'm a perfectionist." "Because I'm afraid to say 'No' to my boss."

See what's happening here? The further down the "why" rabbit hole you go, the closer you get to reality. Keep doing this until you're stuck and all you can say to yourself is "Because!" Odds are, that final quandary points to an aspect of your personal reality worth investigating.

(If you want to stop at five whys, that's your prerogative, but as far as I'm concerned, this can be an all-you-can-why buffet.)

## LET THE FORCES BE WITH YOU

I know I said I was going to focus on the emotional and mental in this chapter, but we still need to give the physical its due because the internal forces that influence your personal reality are largely physical and they have a *huge* impact on your emotional and mental state.

When you get enough sleep, when you eat right, when you exercise, you think better. It's that simple. You make better choices. You perceive the world as a better place. You're better equipped to achieve your Purpose.

■ Sleep helps you make better choices. In fact, a 2011 study from the University of Kansas School of Medicine showed that reducing sleep to seven hours a night resulted in cognitive impairment. When that number went down to five or three hours? Look out . . . This applies to Getting Real because understanding your reality is all about making good choices and deciding which internal and external forces to follow.

■ Food also has a powerful influence on brain function. After all, the brain is an organ like any other. It needs fuel! And with the proper fuel, you function better and live longer. As I said at the start of the chapter, death is inevitable, but we can certainly put the Grim Reaper on standby as we fulfill our Purpose with healthy food and a good night's sleep.

■ Exercise. Really? You're asking *moi* about exercise? Seriously, beyond the myriad other benefits exercise has, it boosts that feel-good hormone serotonin. It makes you happier. And when you're happier, your reality is much brighter. Working out regularly lets you see the world with rose-colored glasses, all the time.

## IGNORING THE BLOCKERS

When a Hider or a New Hater actively tries to stop change in others, he or she becomes a Blocker. A big part of accepting reality is learning how to ignore the negative influence of Blockers. Some days, in the hockey game of life, it feels like every time you try to score, someone whacks the puck back in your face. A huge part of this dilemma stems from our inability to stop caring about what other people think of us. Most of the time, when someone insults you, they aren't thinking about you as much as you think they are. They're just stuck in their own personal reality. We lament for days, weeks, or years over some comment made in passing by someone who forgot what he or she said two minutes after saying it.

But what if they do genuinely have it in for you? If you have a Blocker in your life who doesn't want good things for you, ask yourself, "Why does what they say matter?" Other people's opinions of us are none of your concern. And these particular opinions are their unfinished business, extensions of their own lame internal dialogue.

If you want positive long-term change in life, decide how you're going to influence your personal reality. Let go of your ego and find ways to improve. Life has peaks and valleys, ups and downs, lessons, and celebrations. This is how we grow and learn. Don't let Blockers slam you when you're most vulnerable, at your low points. Instead embrace your external reality and confidently apply your personal reality to it. Both will change for the better.

Like Albert Einstein said, "You can't solve a problem with the same brain that created it." To truly embrace reality is to think outside the situation that created it, and take some risks.

## BE SOLUTION-MINDED

There was a great heist movie that came out a few years back. It involved a group of expert thieves assembled for one last, big job.

They had an amazing plan. It was foolproof. But here's the thing: Once they got going, roadblocks popped up everywhere. They had to spend the whole movie adapting the plan and improvising and coming up with solutions to deal with the onslaught of complications.

Sound familiar? Of course it does, and you know why? *Because that's the plot to every heist movie ever made.* It's also the plot to reality. Roadblocks are a fact of life. There's a lot we can't control, even after we've honed our very best internal forces. While it's important to recognize the reality of a roadblock, placing too much focus on it will derail you. Hiders hide behind roadblocks and use them as excuses. A Hider might show up thirty minutes late for a meeting, flustered and distracted, claiming that it wasn't his fault, because traffic was a bear. Seekers see beyond the immediate block and focus on a solution. If they're late for the meeting, that's okay. There's no point in stressing over how that happened. So when they show up, they walk in cool and in control. They take ownership of the situation by apologizing without excuses. Then they proceed with the task at hand. (But that's the last time they'll be late for a meeting, by the way, because they'll learn from the incident and leave the house earlier next time.)

Let's be honest—we've all hidden behind a roadblock or two. (I live in Los Angeles, where bad traffic is the go-to excuse.) It's easy to shift responsibility; to pass the buck. That's why President Harry S. Truman's motto, "The buck stops here," carried so much impact.

When you pass the proverbial buck, you lose control of your life. You're no longer looking out for your own well-being. You're letting external forces decide how things will turn out—and those forces probably don't have your best interests at heart. What seems like the easy way out actually creates more roadblocks in the long run.

A great metaphor for what I'm talking about is a flat tire. Flats happen. They're Reality 101 when it comes to driving a car. When a Hider gets a flat, he'll spew venom for twenty minutes, outraged that the universe is abusing him (as though he's the only guy who's ever had a flat). Then he'll call the Auto Club, becoming all the more bent out of shape that they're going to take thirty minutes to arrive, as opposed to magically appearing alongside his vehicle like some sort of car-care genie. Meanwhile, he'll use this as an excuse to cancel/delay any unpleasant tasks he has to do that day (even though he'll need to do them eventually). Then, when he finally has it sorted out, he'll drive around on the spare for three months, further tempting fate. The flat didn't suck up all his time—his buck-passing did.

But what does the Seeker do? He just changes the darn tire! He has all the tools in his trunk, so it takes him about fifteen minutes. The next day, he integrates patching the hole into his regular schedule. Ordeal complete.

Focusing on a solution to a problem is daunting. It requires you to quickly put aside any self-pity or excuses. It requires that you think rationally, and not react emotionally. And while it requires you to stay positive, it requires a lot more than positive thinking. When people tell me to "just think positive," I laugh and respond, "That's great, but what's your strategy? How are you going to fix the situation?" It's important to have a good attitude, but just saying the words doesn't mean positive things are going to happen to you. You have to be *proactive* with your positivity. Focus on the solution.

Solution-minded people don't see roadblocks as deal breakers. They're realists, so they know when they've been derailed—but they're practical and they're aware of their capability to cope with the situation. They also have the Big Picture in mind. That roadblock may seem huge at first, but when they hold it up against their Purpose—and the progress they're otherwise making toward that Purpose—it suddenly seems like nothing more than a blip. All this makes them more resilient and willing to do what needs doing. Sometimes they may even see roadblocks as great opportunities to figure something out, to learn something new. They don't listen to Blockers. Instead they just put up a bridge that gets them to the next place.

## CUT YOURSELF A LITTLE SLACK

Let's geek out for a second on some neuroscience. Every time you experience something or learn something—whether it's a new kind of pull-up or a near-miss auto accident—cells in your brain physically change to take on this information. As you go through life, your brain continues to morph as countless synapses are established between cells. In other words, your personality—the sum of your experiences—is a tangible thing, a dense tapestry of connections in your noggin. You are who you are and there's no denying that. Although you can (and should) work to improve yourself, you also need to cut yourself some slack from time to time.

If you're an introvert, you're not going to be the life of the party very often. In fact, you might need to skip a few parties because you need to stay home and recharge your social batteries. You very well might miss that life-changing game of Ultimate Frisbee I mentioned earlier, but that's okay. Just accept who you are. But if one of your goals is to widen your circle of friends, make a plan to go out into the world four times a month. The simple act of showing up will certainly widen that circle.

Or maybe there's something that triggers you into becoming a temporary Hider, making it impossible for you to "let things go." It's important to get to the root of this issue and learn how to avoid it in the future, but if it happens, it happens. By all means, apologize for your behavior and attempt to mend any accidentally burned bridges, but don't beat yourself up. Move on.

In these situations, it's especially helpful to remember to do your best—the best that you can in the moment—and forget about beating yourself up over it.

## THE VALUE OF SELF-TALK

Solution-minded people (aka Seekers) also tend to avoid negative self-talk because it can have a profoundly bad effect on so many aspects of their lives. It influences external forces because when you openly trash yourself, you give the people around you license to do the same.

On the other hand, Seekers embrace having a positive internal conversation. According to the Mayo Clinic, numerous studies show that walking on the sunny side of the street can improve your stress coping skills, impacting psychological issues like depression. Believe it or not, it's also been shown to ward off colds and reduce risk of cardiovascular issues. (It might even wax your floors and wash your dog, but there's not much research on that.)

As I mentioned earlier, a positive attitude is much more than just "staying positive." It's about taking a hard look at your positive attributes—the things that are going to help you succeed—and manifesting those instead of manifesting your negative ones. For example, let's say you don't like your nose. Is that all you are, a nose? Is that your name, the essence of your being? If you took a personality test, would it say "Personality Type: Weird Nose"? Of course not! When thinking and talking about yourself, look beyond that superficial description. Figure out what you are beyond that. Do you have a great smile? Are you a hard worker? Are you compassionate? Are you funny? Are you committed to seeking change? Then that's who you are.

Some of you might be scoffing right now. You're saying, "What's the big deal about a nose? That's not really going to stop anyone from seeing the Big Picture!"

Thank you, Mr. Seeker. You've just proved my point. Whatever it is that makes you talk smack about yourself—be it internal or external—I promise you that it's no bigger a deal than the nose on your face.

The language you use to describe yourself—and others, for that matter—reflects on your ability to see the cup being half full, to search for solutions, and to find answers. In a way, your words are a two-way street. They come from your thoughts, *but they also influence your thoughts.* The words in your brain and the ones coming out of your mouth can serve you or impede you. If you describe yourself as a hard worker, when things get tough you'll be more inclined to roll up your sleeves and get busy. If you describe yourself as a stressed-out basket case, when things get tough you'll throw your hands up in the air in a panic. How do you want to roll? Be conscious of the power of your words, and the effect they have on your reality.

## THE ZEN OF LAUGHTER

It's true that reality sometimes bites. But far too many people see life as a series of brutal obstacles that generate nothing but stress, frustration, and angst. In my own life, I've tried to accept reality as it happens and decipher problems as they emerge, so that the process of figuring things out is an enjoyable one. I am a strong believer that when the going gets tough, you'd better have a sense of humor. I'd rather laugh than cry at some of the ridiculousness that life throws at me.

And it isn't just my opinion that humor is valuable. In fact, a study out of Oxford University showed that the act of laughing—the muscle exertions required to yuk it up—actually releases endorphins, or feel-good hormones, in your brain. What's more, it's healthy to laugh. Over the years, various studies have linked laughter to improved blood flow, a better night's sleep, better immune response, and even improved blood sugar levels.

I'm not saying that you need to a throw a banana cream pie at your husband at breakfast (but send me the YouTube link if you do). I just want you to take it easy on yourself when life gives you lemons. Gallows humor is still humor. Give yourself—and the people around you—the opportunity to smile, laugh, and gain a little perspective.

Believe me, I take the need to laugh very seriously. After all, stand-up comedy was how I first learned the importance of accepting reality. It was the early nineties and I was still teetering between personal training, acting, and a dozen odd jobs. I happened to think I was a reasonably funny guy at the time. Sure, there were some comics who blew my mind, like George Carlin, Steve Martin, Eddie Murphy, and Sam Kinison. Them aside, I thought I could do the job. Piece of proverbial cake, right? I'd be headlining the Comedy Store in no time!

Then reality set in. It turns out that comedy is about ten times harder than it looks. You learn that really quickly when you get up there and you're not getting the responses you thought you were going to get. It didn't exactly go as planned, but I hung in there for a couple of years before I finally realized I was a funnier trainer.

Don't get me wrong; I'm glad I did it. Stand-up is a perfect storm of unpredictable external forces. It was instantly gratifying and instantly terrible at the same time. Depending on the night, depending on the joke, depending on my delivery of the joke—there were so many variables— either I'd get the laugh or I'd get uncomfortable stares from people. It gave me the ultimate chance to experience real life in real time. There's nothing more real than being up onstage completely naked (I mean emotionally, wise guy) without any props, without any musical instruments— just you and a microphone and a bunch of people staring back at you. Sometimes the exchange was brutal, but sometimes it was phenomenal, and that made it all worth it.

And in the long run, the experience had a huge positive impact on my life. Most of my stuff was very animated and physical. (I had one bit involving a gerbil, snow tires, and a tree shredder that used to kill.) Bouncing around onstage delivering those jokes shaped that spontaneous, kinetic kook I became known for as a trainer.

So how does that apply to you and your journey? When you try new things, especially scary things, the reality is that it's going to sting sometimes. When you take big risks, reality is smack-dab in the middle of your face. It can be hard, dirty, and painful. Instead of letting it get you down, you need to keep going with the knowledge that you're giving it all you have; that's all anyone can ask. The reality of my stand-up comedy experience is that it wasn't working for me anymore, so I walked away. Reality will probably teach you the same lesson at some point. Things aren't always going to go as planned. When this happens, be honest with yourself about it. Instead of living in denial or pointing fingers, do what you need to and get on with fulfilling your Purpose.

When you stop fighting reality and just roll with it, life gets so much easier. After all, why do we want life to be different than it is? Reality is who you are and what you're doing, right here, right now. It's the issues we all need to confront every single day. But here's the secret: With every issue you confront, with every obstacle you overcome, life gets a little bit easier. If you're honest and compassionate with yourself and you keep on doing the best you can, you'll find reality can be a pretty incredible place to be.

# LAW 9

## FIND A BALANCE

*Health is a state of complete physical, mental and social well-being and not merely the absence of disease or infirmity.*

—Preamble to the Constitution of the
World Health Organization

By now you should be doing your best to juggle intensity, variety, and consistency—all while keeping your eye on your Purpose and Plan. Sounds like a lot to handle! Luckily, my next law is an easy way to orchestrate all these elements. With balance, you'll be amazed at how many balls you can keep in the air at one time, all while staying focused on the Big Picture.

At its core, balance is as simple as this: If you find yourself focusing too hard on one law, stop, take a breather, and spend some time focusing on another one instead. Let's say you've become incredibly consistent with your eating. Your diet has become a nutritionist's wildest fantasy. Unfortunately, it's also as monotonous as Darth Vader's color scheme. Easy fix—ease up on the consistency a little bit and start upping the variety.

Or maybe you've become a little *too* realistic about your job. You're feeding your cat and paying the bills, but is it feeding your soul and paying credence to your Purpose? No? Well, then maybe it's time to temper that reality and start Loving It a little. Take a chance, make a change, go after something you've always dreamed of pursuing.

In other words, balance is the law that turns the rest of my laws into one big, happy family.

## YIN, MEET YANG

On a philosophical level, finding balance is all about establishing a healthy relationship between our two complementary life forces. The Chinese refer to these opposite energies as Yin and Yang. You probably recognize the symbol below from countless coffee mugs, T-shirts, and, if you run with a certain crowd, tattoos.

The Yin (the white part) represents downtime, relaxation, long walks on the beach, or quiet time spent with a spouse or loved one. Yin energy is restorative. And you need to be restored because the Yang (the black part) represents action, stress, and passion. In other words, Yang kicks butt, takes names, and strives toward your Big Picture goals with all its might. But in the process it can also wear you out. Both sides of the Yin Yang are equally important; you can't have one without the other. The key thing is to maintain a balance between the two that mirrors the little picture above as closely as possible.

In fact, let's take a closer look at the Yin Yang. You'll notice that there is a small black dot in the white half, and a small white dot in the black half. Why is this so? Is it because the original artist wanted to add eyeballs to make the Yin and Yang look like two little tadpoles hugging? Possible but unlikely. The real reason for those dots is to illustrate that these two life energies are equal but not separate. In every Yin, there is a little bit of Yang. And vice versa.

For example, a good workout should be an intense experience for some folks, but there should always be an aspect of fun to it. A solid relationship should make you feel secure and safe, but you need to stay on your toes because if you get *too* comfortable, the whole thing could fall apart. Or here's another one: It's great to have an expert you look up to for advice, but always maintain a small bit of healthy cynicism about what he or she tells you. After all, even mentors are human. (When people come to me for help, I fully expect them to listen with a critical ear.)

The same applies to my laws. By all means, grab one and run with it, but always make sure you have a little fish-eyeball's worth of another law tempering it so that you can maintain perspective.

There are countless ways to define Yin Yang energy, which is probably why the concept has been around for more than three thousand years. Personally, I often see the Yang as physical energy and the Yin as meditative energy. As you may have guessed, I'm a Yang guy, more of a GI Joe than a Ken doll (most of the time, at least). To be honest, balance is not my strong suit. I tend to spend a little too much time bringing it when sometimes I should relax and take a break. Do I need to slow down? Probably, but when I'm bringing it, I'm also Loving It. So maybe, in some situations, Loving It trumps balance. But then again, if what I do works for me, maybe my personal Yin Yang is calibrated slightly differently than most.

## THE VALUE OF YES AND NO

I happen to see my struggle with balance as a "happy problem." Yes, it's important to find a happy medium between your Yin and your Yang. Only problem is, my life is very Yang-centric: I'm always moving and using my physical body, whether that's traveling, teaching a class, or developing and shooting a workout series. I like it—because my Purpose is connected to moving, finding solutions, and taking action. And because I like it, it doesn't create the stress that it would create for other people who may need a little more Yin in their lives.

This is an important point—you have to know your own personal energy balance. While we should all strive to achieve something like the Yin Yang circle, which represents an even distribution of our energies in an effortless flow, the fact is that we are all made of different stuff. Some people love action, love the feeling of being on the move, love the wind in their hair, love being around people. Others love being slow and deliberate, love the quiet, love spending time at home. That's fine. You can have a slightly disproportionate Yin or Yang—*as long as you don't sacrifice one for the benefit of another.*

If I didn't love being such a Yang guy, the energy level required to keep up with my life would exhaust me instead of feeding me. Likewise, if someone with a higher percentage of Yang energy had a boring desk job, they would probably be bouncing off the walls and going out of their minds with frustration. It all goes back to Law 7: Check in and make sure you're Loving It.

Another way I look at Yin and Yang is the balance between saying yes and no. I had a tremendous lack of balance in that sense when I was younger. I said no to everything. "No" was practically my middle name. But today, I like to think I've become Tony "Yes" Horton. Life is filled with opportunities that I'm ready to participate in. I had opportunities as a kid but I wasn't mentally, emotionally, and physically ready for them so "no" it was. I wasn't willing to go through the learning experience. Fear dictated my lack of balance.

And while I do push myself, I know when to draw the line. Because saying yes too often can also create an imbalance. Case in point: I never say yes to anything that would cause me to miss my morning workout. It's physical, of course, but it's also what helps me feel calm and focused for the rest of the day. Everything else in my life gets scheduled around that time because it is vital to me. And if that means saying no to a few things that can't be rescheduled, so be it. Imbalance happens when you say no to an opportunity that you intuitively know is going to give you a better, happier life.

I do struggle with saying no in some instances where I know I'm already burning the candle at both ends, but the truth is, at this stage in my life I feel very lucky to have the opportunities that have been offered to me, and it almost feels criminal to say no to anything. As a result I sometimes I get burnout. As I write this book, I'm designing new programs for Beachbody, I'm juggling three or four other projects, and I'm traveling like a maniac. I probably should have said no to some of the traveling.

In fact, I did have to say no to a trip to Afghanistan and Iraq recently. It was a heartbreaker. I love meeting our troops, but I needed to draw the line somewhere; otherwise I'd show up in the Middle East burned out and exhausted. I don't think that would inspire anyone. "Hi, I'm Tony Horton. Mind if I borrow your cot? I need some Yin time." Not the vibe of a great motivator.

So the lesson is twofold. Don't say no when it comes from fear or laziness, therefore ruining your opportunities to say yes. The second part I'm still working on: Do say no when it comes from a need to take care of yourself, therefore increasing your opportunities to say yes.

## THINK OF BALANCE AS A TEETER-TOTTER

Balance doesn't mean sitting under the Bodhi tree all day, aligned with the universe like some kind of modern-day Buddha wannabe. The goal of balance is no more about perfection than the goal of fitness is to have a six-pack. The goal of balance is to take advantage of opportunities for growth, to know your abilities and your limits, to protect yourself from harm, and not to get in your own way.

Think of finding balance as like riding a teeter-totter. You don't just sit there, perfectly balanced, parallel to the ground.

Sure, there's a balance *point*, but there are energies on either end that make it go up and down, which is part of the ride.

Imbalance happens when one end is too heavy, when a four-hundred-pound gorilla climbs on with nobody on the other end. But if there's a kid on each side, it's perfectly normal for things to teeter and totter. Constant adjustment is the name of the game. You may not be in balance 100 percent of the time, but as long as you're aware of what's off-kilter and you take strides to adjust it, you're on the right path.

## HOW BALANCED ARE YOU?

Now that we've mastered the basics of balance, let's think about how it breaks down in terms of the Big Picture. For that, we'll need a different illustration. After all, the Yin Yang may feature two forces—but you have a lot more forces than that in your life! So instead of redrawing the Yin Yang to look like some kind of pizza divided into slices on a Tilt-A-Whirl, let's look to another helpful tool for thinking about how to achieve balance in multiple areas of your life. It's called a Venn diagram (remember this from eighth grade?).

This particular Venn diagram features three overlapping circles: Exercise, Nutrition, and Rest. As you can see on the next page, while they are all distinct categories, they are also interconnected. Exercise allows you to sleep better; and when you're well rested, you're more likely to have a good workout. Healthy food fuels your exercise, and a good diet allows you to get good-quality sleep; and resting aids digestion.

And then, at the heart of the matter, they all intersect, because these three things are the cornerstones of wellness.

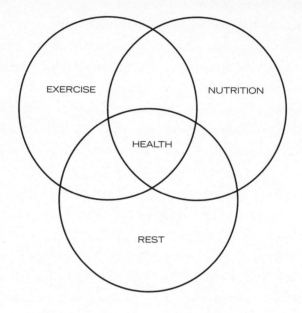

Not only do the overlapping circles suggest how one part of your life can benefit another; they can also suggest how one aspect can *detract* from another. So if, for example, you've been feeling fatigued quickly in your workouts, it may mean that something's wrong with your diet—maybe you're not getting enough calories, carbs, or protein. Or it could be that rest is the issue. Or stress issues could be getting in your way. The point is that the solution is to find the imbalance—and that imbalance isn't always going to be in the obvious place.

This particular Venn diagram may seem a little obvious, but you can use this approach for just about any aspect of your life to gain some insight about balance. Your relationship may be on the fritz, but is it purely because of the two of you? Relationships don't exist in a vacuum, so maybe something connected to your relationship, such as your work, your past, or your friends, is impacting it.

Here's how to create your own Venn diagram:

1. On a piece of paper, write down, *in pencil*, the aspect of your life that lacks balance and draw a big circle around it.

2. Think of all the other parts of your life that might influence this one area and write them down. Draw circles around each of these words. If a word represents a smaller part of your life, draw a small circle around it. If it represents a bigger part of your life, draw a large circle around it. The more each of these areas impacts the issue you're trying to sort out, the more it should overlap with your main circle.

3. Think about the connections. Because you're using pencil, don't be afraid to erase and move circles around as you make new connections.

4. When you notice an especially large overlap, spend some time focusing on how the two parts of your life influence each other positively and negatively. I guarantee you'll find issues to work on.

The upshot of this is that whatever the problem is, there's always a solution, so if what you're doing isn't working, it's just a matter of trying something else. Finding balance is like finding lost car keys. It can be elusive, but it's there somewhere. Key fairies didn't sneak into your home in the middle of the night and steal your keys—or your balance, for that matter. It's just a matter of taking inventory and searching in unexpected places before you find them.

# LIVE IN THE MOMENT

When I first moved to California, people used to tell me to "be present" and "live in the moment."

At the time, I had no idea what those silly granola-eaters were talking about. What moment? Of course I'm in the moment! Where else would I be? Yesterday? The Old West? Milwaukee?

Today I know what both of those expressions mean and they've had a huge impact on my life. They're more than just Left Coast actor-speak. In fact, you can achieve balance only when you're present and living in the moment.

Because in order to be balanced, you have to have an awareness of what it is you're doing *right now*. How can you know if your balance is off-kilter if you're mindlessly going through the motions? Likewise, how can you assess anything in your life accurately if you're preoccupied with the past or the future? So many people are stuck in the past, stressing out about what they coulda, shoulda, woulda done or about what they feel has been done to them. Others spend all their time thinking about the future—worrying about it, fearing it, or creating unrealistic expectations for themselves. How many times have you heard someone say, "If only I could (make more money/meet my soul mate/lose ten pounds/move to a new house or city), my life would be so much better"?

Does all this past and future thinking fuel success? Not at all. It just adds clutter that gets in the way of focusing on our Big Picture goals. Of course, it's important to learn from the past, but keep it in perspective. You learned all kinds of great things in school, right? (And a lot of useless stuff too, for the record.) Does that mean you'd be better off walking around with all your old textbooks strapped to your back? Of course not. *Learn the lessons your past offers, but leave the baggage behind.*

Same with the future. Sure, it's fun to look forward to tomorrow's adventures and to plan and dream and fantasize, but when you focus too much on what your life should or could look like five years from now, you can't really participate in what it looks like now.

These days, being present in the moment is more difficult than ever because there are so many distractions at our fingertips. If you're not in this moment, what happens? If you're focused on the past or the future, then you're going to be missing out on the essence of life and the Big Picture.

## HEY, GANG! LET'S MEDITATE!

I can almost see the collective eye-roll. "Tony's meditating now? Please don't tell me he's getting all woo-woo on me!"

Relax. A third eye hasn't sprouted out of my forehead (yet). And I'm much too fond of my hair for the Buddhist monk look (plus it's hard to wear flowy robes when I'm climbing the rope). I just want to help you add a little more balance to your life.

Meditation may seem mystical to some, but it's a completely secular (nonreligious) practice that's backed by all kinds of science. For example, a study published in the journal *Circulation: Cardiovascular Quality and Outcomes* showed that people with coronary heart disease who meditated reduced their risk of heart attack, stroke, or death by 48 percent. Not 4 percent, but 48 percent.

Loosely speaking, your nervous system is divided into two parts: the sympathetic nervous system and the parasympathetic system. Even though the sympathetic nervous system sounds soft and fuzzy (*sympathetic*, like with ponies and rainbows, right?), it's actually the "fight or flight" part of your nervous system and it activates cortisol, the stress hormone we talked about back in chapter 7. The parasympathetic nervous system is the part that maintains the stuff we do unconsciously, like digestion and sexual arousal. Some people call it the "rest and digest system." So when your nervous system is out of balance and you spend too much time fighting or fleeing, your resting and digesting suffer.

Meditation helps bring your nervous system back into balance by upping your parasympathetic activity—making it another useful tool alongside Loving It for fighting excess cortisol. A Harvard Medical School study used MRI technology to reveal that meditation activates the autonomic nervous system (the larger umbrella for the parasympathetic and sympathetic nervous systems), which plays a huge part in warding off heart disease, digestive problems, and infertility.

How amazing is that? I'm not talking about worshipping a golden elephant or a brass monkey. I'm talking about taking a few minutes every day to stop, sit, and quiet the crazy monologue in your head that only adds stress to your hectic life.

## My Meditation Practice

I'm what you might call a "recreational meditator." If you're looking for a heavy-duty meditation guru, check out the appendixes at the back of this book—there are some really great guides out there. But if you're just looking to dip your toe in the meditation pool, my practice is perfect for beginners.

First, find someplace comfortable where you feel relaxed and mellow. (No, I don't mean your bed. Meditation works best when you sit up straight and avoid falling asleep.)

My meditation spot is a redwood bench in my backyard. It looks out over the whole city. I can see the San Gabriel Mountains, Westwood, Brentwood, and the Hollywood sign. It's a beautiful place to be.

Next, set aside ten or fifteen minutes with no distractions. At first, you might not make it through the whole time because your brain might be jumping all over the place. That's okay. The Law of Consistency works here. Just show up and, eventually, sitting still for that long will come more easily to you. My meditation time maxes out at about fifteen minutes, which isn't very long, but it gets the job done.

I start with my hands folded in my lap and a notepad, pen, and timer next to me. I close my eyes, let the sun bake my sunscreened face, and breathe. I *try* to keep my mind clear. When thoughts do pop into my head—inevitably that's just going to happen—I try to ignore them, typically by focusing on my breath.

If that doesn't work—if a thought is especially strong—I use the bubble trick. I surround the thought in one of those cartoon talking bubbles and imagine popping it. Most times it works and when it doesn't, it wasn't supposed to. That's meditation for me.

Now, this is where my practice is a little different. While I'm happy to burst the unproductive thought bubbles, sometimes good-idea thoughts pop up that I'd like to remember. Thoughts that can help me solve the things I'm working on or worried about. When this happens, I stop the meditation and write them down.

A lot of meditation is aimed at completely clearing your mind, but I sometimes use it more as a way of getting clarity. It's an opportunity to get rid of the chaff and focus on the wheat, a great way to help me deal with some of the issues in my life.

But there's a trick to it. I never sit down and say, "Today, I'm going to solve problem X." On the contrary, I'm just trying to chill, but good things happen sometimes when you least expect them.

I'm not a chanter, but some people add that to their meditation. Some get fancy and use Buddhist chants like *nam-myoho-renge-kyo*. Others just say *Breathe in. Breathe out.* Find a phrase that makes you feel good. It can be *I like bananas and chocolate*, if you want. Or simply, traditionally, *Om*.

There are a million ways to meditate and all of them are correct, so don't get lost in getting it perfect. Just sit your butt down and let go. The rest will just come to you.

## MEET THE EXPERTS

### Ted McDonald, aka Mr. Meditation

I first met Ted McDonald a few years back when I was discovering yoga. I'd heard about his class at Maha Yoga in the Brentwood section of Los Angeles, and he was known for his inversions—shoulder stands, headstands, handstands, etc. He was an upside-down kind of guy, and I desperately wanted to learn how to do a handstand. I went to him because I knew he'd have insight on how to do one properly.

As it turned out, he was also a snowboarder who held yoga retreats all over the world. I signed up for my first Ted McDonald Adventure Yoga Retreat in Mammoth, California. It was the first time I got to know the guy, and we bonded over the love of the mountains and sun salutations. Since then we've run four retreats together, from Tuscany to Chamonix.

Since then he's become a valuable yoga guru for me, playing a huge role in creating the sequences in P90X2 and other workouts. Ted has also been meditating for years, and has found a way to combine his loves for yoga, long-distance running, and a tranquil mind. I'm just glad to know the guy because he's taught me how to see the world and step outside my comfort zone.

**TONY:** How did you come into meditation?

**TED:** I started seeking some kind of spiritual solution back in my late teens because I was dating someone who died suddenly of spinal meningitis. We were making plans to see each other when, next thing I knew, I got a call that she was gone. This young woman, she was beautiful, a straight-A student, she had everything going for her and all of the sudden she's ripped from this planet.

**TONY:** Wow. I'm sorry.

**TED:** Thanks. So, I started this search and got into Buddhism a little bit. And one of the main things of Buddhism is meditation. So for a long time, my form of meditation was really just coming home from a busy day, lying on my bed, turning on some cool music, lighting a candle, and creating this ambience. That was it. But I was never able to sit in silence for a long time. And then a few years later, I had an addiction issue I had to get a handle on, so I went cold turkey. At that point, I needed to dial up the meditation because I was feeling like I was crazy.

**TONY:** How'd that work out for you?

**TED:** One of the fundamentals of meditation is to have a straight spine, because the energy flows through your body and you want to be upright so that the energy can flow that way. So I sat down in a chair, lit a candle, set my timer, and tried to sit for ten minutes. Five minutes into it, I started freaking out. I started shivering and shaking. It was so intense for me because my mind was going so quickly, you know? I couldn't even do ten minutes.

**TONY:** How do you meditate? Are you emptying your mind or just letting it wander?

**TED:** I think that's what holds people back from meditation. People get so freaked-out by it because they believe that you're supposed to empty your mind. But that's a cliché. *What you resist persists.* So if you force your mind to be empty, it's like "I'm going to tell you not to think about a monkey."

**TONY:** Great. Now I'm thinking about a damn monkey.

**TED:** Right? There are three fundamentals I teach people about meditation. One is to have a straight spine. Two is a relaxed breath. Three is what they call a "single-pointed focus."

Depending on your mind of meditation, that can be the third eye center—that energy center in between the eyebrows. It can be the heart center—the energy center in the middle of your chest—it can be the beach, it can be the top of a mountain. It just needs to be some place for you that makes sense, that feels peaceful.

It doesn't matter what you choose because what it does is it gives the mind a place to go. Inevitably, you're going to have twenty thousand different thoughts going around. So if we follow them all, it's basically the tail wagging the dog; we're following this crazy thought pattern.

Giving your mind a place to go is an exercise. If you stick with it, eventually all those twenty thousand different thoughts that are going on at the same time slow down. They become ten thousand and then five thousand and then one thousand and then slowly but surely you become more aware of your breathing, the energy that moves through your body, your sensations, and ultimately you become aware of the moment. That's the idea in meditation, not to shut off, but to get totally aware and present in the moment.

**TONY:** How do you live in the moment and still plan for the future and achieve things?

**TED:** What happens is that you live in two worlds. You live in the moment as much as you can, experiencing the moment and also planning your life and what you want to do. The two work together because you focus on what you're doing now, as it pertains to the future.

For example, right now I'm planning what I'm going to do for the future because I'm getting married. So we have to make reservations and we have to design save-the-dates and we have to meet with the DJ and all those kinds of things. But when I'm meeting with the DJ, I'm not thinking about the fact that I'm going to go to dinner afterward. I'm there with the DJ. You need to find a balance—unless you're going to go live in a cave. Then you can be in the moment the whole time.

I think in our society, the goal of meditation is not to empty the mind because I think that causes people too much havoc. Simply calm the mind a little bit, find some solace in our chaotic world away from information and Internet and emails and jobs and all that sort of stuff. It's nice to decompress.

**TONY:** One trick I like to use in meditating is to write everything down. When it's in there it doesn't have to be in my head. That allows me to live in the moment. Is that a practice you ever use?

**TED:** That's a practice I always use! I thank God for my iPhone because now I don't have to carry a pen and paper. My iPhone is basically my head dump.

**TONY:** Occasionally, I hear more pious types express concern that they might go to hell if they start meditating. How do you respond to that kind of thinking?

**TED:** I would say no, we're definitely not going to go to hell for meditating. You don't even have to call it meditation. When you just sit quietly and observe your breathing, relax, and focus on one point, eventually all your external thoughts slow down and you get to really observe and listen to your inner voice. Some people call it your sixth sense or your intuition, but for some people, religious people, that's God, right? So don't even use the word "meditation." For some people it's more about calming the mind and tapping into the God within.

**TONY:** What if you're already on top of the world? Why would someone cruising happily through life need meditation?

**TED:** I think anyone could benefit from getting quiet a little bit. We've all got so much going on. You can seem to be pretty self-sufficient and cruising, but it's always nice to just take some time, let things clear out. That way, you can be more productive.

**TONY:** So you're really talking about balance. Yin and Yang.

**TED:** Absolutely. The Yin and the Yang.

## BALANCING THE BODY

Because of the way meditation cuts through stress, it's a great tool for both the mind and body. In fact, most mind de-stressing techniques tend to benefit your whole body, since the two are connected in countless ways, ranging from your nervous system to your endocrine system to something as simple as the tension in your neck.

So far in this chapter, I've focused on techniques that balance your noggin with the knowledge that they'll have a trickle-down influence on your body. Now let's upend the equation and discuss finding balance for your body, understanding that this will ultimately help your head as well.

The vast majority of people who work out don't have a ton of balance in their regime; they figure that if they just commit, work hard, and show up, that's the whole battle. And that is a big piece of it. But they're probably missing a number of circles in that Venn diagram we looked at earlier. One- or two-dimensional fitness just doesn't cut the mustard the same way multidimensional fitness does. As I often say, the future of fitness is about speed, balance, and range of motion.

People always ask me how, at fifty-five years old, I manage to stay uninjured most of the time. A big part of it is because I try to incorporate balance in many of my workouts. For example, I never work my legs more than three times a week, just as I wouldn't train my upper body every single day, either. It's as simple as working lower body on a Monday and Wednesday and upper body on a Tuesday and Thursday so each half of the system has a chance to rest, repair, heal, and grow.

Then I take it further and throw a bunch of other techniques and methods into the mix—core and functional days, plyometric leg-pounding days, yoga days. Sometimes I lift weights and sometimes I don't. My workouts are about what I need, not what some fitness dogma dictates. I don't care what all the cool kids are doing—even if they're training by lifting eighty-pound sacks of bat guano. I'm going to do whatever seems like the right thing to do on that particular day.

It's about finding balance in my workout so that I can continue to get better without boredom, plateaus, or injuries. (Especially without injuries. Not a fan of those.) That's what the P90X series is about, because it's just the way I train.

## A FEW BALANCING TOOLS

I can hear some of you shouting, "Oh no! What if I'm out of balance? What do I do?"

Relax. Your legs aren't going to fall off tomorrow. Remember, balance isn't about being perfect. It's about noticing the areas in your life that need fixing and working on them. It might be that your hamstrings are too tight or your hamburgers are too many. Whatever it is, the moment you start trying to make things work better, you've started improving your own balancing act.

If you're looking for some tools to add balance to your workouts, Variety is your first stop. A variety of different workouts is the only way to become a well-rounded athlete. It's also the ideal way to prevent—say it with me now—*boredom, plateaus, and injuries.* Second, you need flexibility, which we'll discuss in depth in chapter 10. Here is the CliffsNotes version: Flexibility helps you realize when something you're doing isn't working so that you can try something else. Staying rigid in your regimen is a recipe for imbalance, in mind and body.

I also highly recommend you get yourself a foam roller and start rolling out those knots and tight muscles today. Quads, iliotibeal (IT) bands, calves, hip flexors, glutes, lats, pecs—if it's made of muscle and it's attached to your body, roll it out.

Finally, there are my Three R's: Rest, Recover, and Relax (more on these in chapter 11!). Exercise is reflected in the Yin Yang, too—the other half of activity is inactivity. Remember all those times I've told you to get off your couch and exercise? Note that *I never told you to get rid of that couch*. I have four couches in my house and I have to admit that I use them regularly. An important aspect of balance is knowing when to take it easy.

## YOGA: MOVING MEDITATION

If I had to choose one type of fitness for the rest of my life, it would be yoga. To me, it's the perfect balance between Yin and Yang, balance, strength, and flexibility.

Personally, I prefer Hatha yoga. It has a flow that gives my mind and body an opportunity to work synergistically. But don't take my word for it—try them all. Hatha, Iyengar, Kundalini, even Yin yoga. Actually, a lot of yoga styles have converged anyway (not unlike rock and roll). The yogi teaching a class can also wildly influence a practice. So try a few different forms with a few different instructors before throwing in your sweat-drenched towel. If you keep looking, you'll find the perfect balance.

## IMBALANCE AND OVERCOMPENSATION

Everything in your body is interconnected, including your bones, muscles, tendons, ligaments, and all the other parts you use to exercise. (We call this the kinetic chain.) When one part isn't functioning properly, it can cause a system-wide breakdown, so your body compensates by strengthening another part to make up for it. While this sounds like a pretty slick fix-it, it can quickly turn into an issue. The injured part continues to erode while the part (or parts) overcompensating for it and doing the extra work becomes taxed or overdeveloped. A classic example is that when you have tight hamstrings, your quadriceps beef up to pick up the slack. You'll get by at first, but over time those hamstrings can cause other injuries, usually in the lower back. Furthermore, because your legs aren't functioning the way they should, they're also not functioning *as well* as they should. If you fixed those hamstrings, you could jump higher, run fast, and be less prone to injury.

When the physical aspects of your life come together, you feel better. And when you feel better, your mental state improves. What's more, not only does exercise release a cascade of feel-good hormones, but it also gives you time to think—or not think (depending on what you need).

A balanced body is a less painful body. And when you're not focused on pain, it's so much easier to do the thinking—or not thinking—I mentioned above. Over the years, I've gained tons of emotional and mental clarity during my workouts. In fact, I've formulated much of my Big Picture philosophy in the gym or on the slopes.

The nice thing about including exercise in your mental balance toolbox is that it's a tool that practically uses itself. When you work out, you can't help but improve what's going on in your head.

## Steve Holmsen, a Class Balancing Act

Trainer/ski instructor extraordinaire Steve Holmsen has been a pain in my butt since the day I met him. He's also been a pain in my hip flexors, IT bands, thighs, and calves. You see, Steve's the guy who turned me onto self-myofascial release, a self-massage therapy that uses a foam roller or a medicine ball to massage out the knots in your body. It's painful when you start, to say the least. But once you've worked out tension that's been building in your muscles for decades, it makes life pretty wonderful.

But Steve's gig goes beyond that; he's a true Big Picture thinker. His goal is to help people train their biomechanical systems to work better, to work pain-free. He realizes that if you know how to use your body properly, you can do almost anything. "You can level that playing field," he says. "It's not like when you were younger and certain people got picked for certain sports because they were natural athletes. I get people who think they aren't very good at sports, and when you change their movement patterns, suddenly they're great athletes. In other words, everybody has the ability to be a great athlete."

**TONY:** What opened your eyes to the importance of balance in physical movement?

**STEVE:** My wife, Jennifer, played a big part. She's also a trainer. She teaches Pilates and she studied exercise science in college. She was the first one who really pointed out to me that I had horrendous movement patterns. I had no idea how to squat properly, no idea how to fire the right muscles in the right sequence.

I was almost getting a little nervous about getting older because I was thinking to myself, "Wow, I've got this joint pain here and this other issue here" and everybody's saying, "Oh, you know, as you get older you're going to have these issues." Then I realized, no, it's because my movement patterns were poor and they were creating shearing and compressive forces on my joints.

**TONY:** Which joints specifically were problematic?

**STEVE:** Knees. I had two knee surgeries in the early nineties. They tried to repair my torn meniscus. So I think I was non-weight-bearing for a couple of months and had no lateral motion for half a year. Then I tore it again and they took out most of it.

**TONY:** So you could have avoided those surgeries with proper movement patterns.

**STEVE:** Yes. I realized that it's such a foundational movement because I have a son, Adam, who is twenty-three months old. He has perfect squat mechanics. His hips go back perfectly, his weight's on his calcaneus [heel bone]. It's remarkable. Nobody ever taught him that. Just genetically he knows how to do that. It's fascinating watching that because you realize that within everybody is an athlete.

Often when people work out, they're not really able to discern whether they're actually taxing their muscles or putting pressure on their joints. We often just get so used to it and assume, "Oh, that's just my body. There's not really a solution to that." There are solutions to all sorts of issues in all sorts of bodies.

**TONY:** Is there more to making those corrections than just telling someone how to move?

**STEVE:** I think more often than not, in order to learn, there almost has to be some kind of blow to your ego—especially for males. When I got into yoga, I was determined to do the hardest poses even though I wasn't even close to ready for them; I needed to do the remedial ones. But my ego prevented me from actually doing it in the correct sequence. And that's one of the reasons that the exercises that I develop for people do actually mess with somebody's ego.

**TONY:** So you need to break someone down physically and mentally to build them back up again?

**STEVE:** When I teach ski lessons, I have these guys who say, "I want to go ski that double-black terrain," and I could even tell just by how they walked, how they carried their skis, how they traversed—they weren't ready. I'd say, "I can get you to that level if we work on a couple of skills that'll allow you to do that." They'd say, "Oh, no, I don't want to work on those skills. I want to go there."

I'd say, "Okay," and we'd go to the difficult terrain. I can make it look easy and effortless. They struggle, get scared, and then they come back to me and say, "Can we work on that stuff that you mentioned so I can learn how to do that as well as you just did it?"

Often somebody has to come around on their own terms, which is fine. The terrain essentially tames them and teaches them.

**TONY:** Sometimes, progress isn't pretty.

**STEVE:** Yeah, like when I first exposed you to stability ball and medicine ball exercises and all the different balance challenges out there. You hated it because you were horrible.

**TONY:** I was horrible? "Horrible" is a strong word.

**STEVE:** Either way, we often hate what we stink at. We want to be good at everything right away. We figure, "I'm fit! I should be able to do this, no problem." That's another reason why I design the exercises the way I do. If you learn to really cultivate your balance you will actually be good at pretty much everything you do.

If you learn proper movement patterns and learn to fire the right muscles in the right sequence and neurologically change how that happens, then you'll naturally become a better athlete because you're not fighting your own body.

Once you have excellent movement patterns, then you can focus on a sport. If somebody is lacking essential movement patterns, they're always going to falter. And that's happened to a number of top athletes. Tiger Woods had to change his swing. Kobe Bryant's knees would go in and forward when he used to jump, which is the ideal scenario for an ACL tear. He had to change that.

**TONY:** Even sports stars need balance to achieve The Big Picture.

**STEVE:** That's my big picture, too! So I mean in some respects I'm tolerant because I love working with people, I don't care how in shape they are or how many issues they have. In my opinion, every human has a responsibility to take care of him- or herself.

# LAW 10

## STAY FLEXIBLE

*When we are no longer able to change a situation, we are challenged to change ourselves.*

—Viktor E. Frankl

There's a story I like to tell because it illustrates just how essential flexibility is to being part of the Big Picture. One Friday afternoon—an afternoon like any other—ten people were waiting in line at a local bank, depositing paychecks, getting some cash for the weekend, stuff we all do from time to time. Suddenly two masked men burst through the front door, knocking out the security guard, waving guns, and yelling for everyone to get down, faces to the floor. They made a point of dialing up the fear factor, firing off the occasional round as they pressed their heels into the back of the prone customers' necks, ripping off personal effects—watches, necklaces—and shouting threats.

When the robbers made their escape (they were never caught,

incidentally), everyone was shaken. More important, however, they were alive.

But the story doesn't end there. If we follow the victims for the next five years, we see that the event affected them in very different ways. Some of them struggled to recover from the trauma of the incident. They simply couldn't come to terms with the fact that something like this could happen to them. They suffered from night terrors, paranoia, and depression. Some of their marriages buckled under the strain. Others lost their jobs because the tiniest hint of stress triggered them in the workplace. Many of them began taking medications to deal with their crippling anxiety. Their lives became marked forever as "before" and "after" the robbery.

Others were also affected, but they turned to counseling, prayer, exercise, or other coping tools to work though the trauma. It took a lot of hard work, but these people came out on the other side relatively unscathed. They returned to their lives relatively quickly. The event stayed with them, but they were able to leave it in the past and move forward.

Why did some people recover from this incident while others didn't? Because some people were flexible enough to adapt. I'm grateful that I've never experienced anything like this and I hope you haven't, either. But we'll all experience trauma at some point in our lives, whether it's a robbery, a car accident, illness, divorce, or the death of a loved one. When this happens, it's important to have the flexibility to accept it and do the work that's required to deal with it.

Acceptance is a much harder path through pain than denial, but it's the only way to come out the other side. In fact, some mental health experts even believe that it's possible to *benefit* from traumatic events. The concept is called "post-traumatic growth" and it's about digging deeper inside yourself in a way that can help you strengthen relationships, discover new opportunities, gain a deeper appreciation for life, trigger spiritual growth, and sharpen your focus on the Big Picture.

Resilience isn't just key to happiness; it's key to success. When you Get Real, you understand that misfortune is part of life. When it comes your way, facing it head-on is the only way you'll be able to continue toward your Purpose.

## IT'LL ONLY MAKE YOU STRONGER

I'm not trying to be a Pollyanna here. Really tragic, horrible things happen to good people. But what happens afterward is where flexibility matters. Take Tammy Duckworth, the U.S. senator from Illinois. When she lost both her legs serving in the Iraq War, she could have just come home, retired, and stopped fighting the good fight. A lot of people would have. Instead, she became even more focused in her devotion to her country and ran for office as a public servant.

Another amazing example of post-traumatic growth is the man whose quote appears at the beginning of this chapter, Viktor Frankl. His book *Man's Search for Meaning* chronicles his experiences as a prisoner in the Nazi concentration camp Auschwitz during World War II. He survived the experience by looking deep inside himself, finding meaning in the middle of the horrors that he was subjected to. He went on to write a book that would change the lives of countless people (including mine). As he puts it, "Everything can be taken from a man but one thing: the last of the human freedoms—to choose one's attitude in any given set of circumstances, to choose one's own way." In other words, Viktor Frankl chose to survive—and as a result, it gave his life an incredibly powerful Purpose.

I'm awed and inspired by people who are able to rise from the ashes and turn their misfortune into a blessing, who rebound from tragedy and then go on to effect positive change in the world. No matter how bad things get, the only way to not just survive but to *thrive*, is to embrace the wisdom offered by Frankl. Even when it feels like you've lost control of everything, you haven't—you have a choice of how you respond to any given situation.

## FUNCTIONAL OPTIMISM

How do you perform under pressure? In chapter 8, when we discussed Getting Real, we looked at two different kinds of reality—that which is internal, or controlled by you, and that which is external, or controlled by the outside world. Most traumatic situations are part of your *external* reality. As I like to say, the situation is the situation, so how are you going to react to it? Odds are very high that it's not going to magically change just because you want it to. Your personal reality, on the other hand, is highly pliable. Like Frankl, those who rise to the occasion under tough circumstances succeed by looking inside themselves, at their personal reality, for the solution. They make a point of being flexible.

But when you're being flexible it's also important to bend *the right way*. If you decide you're a victim of circumstance, then that's what you'll be. It's not that misfortune will be magically drawn your way; it's that you'll expect bad things to happen, and so you'll be more inclined to focus on and remember the negative things that come your way. Furthermore, focusing on negative emotions reinforces those thought patterns (like creating a bad habit instead of a good one), leading you into a downward spiral of frustration and depression.

So when obstacles pop up, it's important to recognize the need to deal with them realistically, with a plan, but one that is born from a positive mind-set. I call this Functional Optimism and it's a key component of achieving your Big Picture goals. It's not about knowing everything can work out. It's about knowing that everything will work out *because you're going to do what you need to do to make it happen.*

## THE FOUNTAIN OF YOUTH

Spanish conquistador Juan Ponce de León had it all wrong tearing up the New World in search of the Fountain of Youth. If he'd just had a consistent yoga practice, he never would have had to leave Spain.

While being flexible with your mind allows you to grow and be more resilient emotionally, adding flexibility work to your fitness regime allows you to be resilient physically. Flexibility is the cornerstone of any worthwhile exercise program because it allows you to move how you want to move. And when you combine the two—mental and physical flexibility—they allow you to live the way you want to live.

Physical flexibility increases your range of motion and makes you less prone to the snaps and tears that tight muscles and tendons can cause. In other words, it protects you from trauma and injury. Building flexibility—through regular stretching and exercise like yoga—is important for everyone, but it becomes essential as we grow older. Aging has a funny way of making everything we do harder, in part because we grow less flexible with age. On average, we lose up to 50 percent mobility in some joints by the time we hit our golden years. What's so golden about that? And who wants to live out their retirement years like the Tin Man? Not me.

## BACK IN THE DAY . . .

When I was a young lad, no one really talked about stretching. When I heard the word "yoga," I thought people were mispronouncing "yogurt." Come to think of it, I didn't know what yogurt was, either . . . (I've since seen the light.)

In gym class back in the sixties there were fitness test benchmarks that determined how capable you were: push-ups, pull-ups, dips, sit-ups (not crunches), the hundred-yard dash, and touching your toes. The first five items on the list involved strength or speed. Some kids had it, while others did not. (I was in the "did not" category.) On the other hand, touching your toes was a breeze for all of us. Even out-of-shape kids like me could touch their toes. We didn't have to deal with tight hamstrings. We didn't even know what hamstrings were. I could have talked your ear off about Ponce de León, but had you asked, I would have guessed hamstrings were some kind of pig jerky.

When you're young, you're naturally flexible and likely to recover quickly. Kids get scrapes, bruises, even broken bones, but it's pretty rare for children to pull a muscle, and if they do, they recover in the blink of an eye. Back in the good old days, the focus was on running faster and jumping higher. The only kids in my neighborhood who stretched were gymnasts or ballerinas—and they were just doing it to show off.

## YOGA: IT'S CHILD'S PLAY!

I often tell people that if I could do only one type of workout, it would be yoga—and that's not just because I'm in my fifties and looking to stay flexible. When you're younger, it's true that you're more flexible, but it's crucial to nurture that natural gift because if you don't use it, you'll lose it. After all, the problems that come with age, the tight muscles and bad backs, are just around the corner. You—and/or your kids—may as well head them off at the pass. Furthermore, yoga helps youngsters with its less obvious benefits, such as mental clarity, recovery, and detoxification. (I know you feed your kids healthy foods that they don't necessarily need to detox from but, hey, Froot Loops happen, right?)

Unfortunately, slashed budgets are crushing school physical education programs, so many kids hardly get the chance to squeeze in a daily game of outlawed dodgeball, let alone yoga. Luckily, Big Picture thinking can come to the rescue. I know a few honorable yoga instructors who volunteer to teach in schools. In fact, my collaborator Denis's nine-year-old daughter, Cassidy, is practically a yogini herself, thanks to her after-school yoga program. She frequently lectures her chronically stiff dad on the importance of keeping his back leg straight during the warrior series.

Do you think teaching yoga—or any other physical activity—at your local school might be part of your Plan? I hope so! With any luck, today's limber kids won't have tomorrow's tight hamstrings and tweaked lower backs.

# MY FIRST YOGA CLASS

No one taught yoga at Daniels Farm Elementary in 1968. Even if they did, I would have had no interest in learning how to say "Om" or stand on my head, so I learned the benefits of flexibility relatively late in life. It was the early nineties and, as happened with quite a few things during that time, I discovered it because I was looking for love—specifically, a very bendy blonde. I'd known about yoga for quite a while but hadn't done the research to know what it was, what benefits it might offer—and I certainly hadn't tried it. But just like most uninformed people, I had an opinion about it anyway—a negative one. I thought it was silly and it looked too easy to bother with. I assumed my first class would be a waste of my time and I'd have to do a "real" workout afterward to make up for this faux fitness. But there was a chance I might score a few points with my future wife, so I showed up anyway. That "PX90" tough guy with his panoply of fitness know-how was going to get in there and show those hippies how it was done (and win the girl at the same time).

Ten minutes into the class, I was streaming sweat like a lawn sprinkler with a thyroid condition. I was shaking, rattling, and rolling around like a real rookie. My downward-facing dog was more like a Halloween cat. My shoulders were tight, my spine wasn't flexible, and my hamstrings were hamstrung.

I didn't get the girl but the experience was so impactful that I added yoga into my weekly routine, and it's been that way ever since. Despite my struggle, I felt amazing after that class. A regular yoga practice stretches you out, releases tension, and promotes blood flow. And it does wonders for your mental state. It's well documented that yoga can help with everything from depression to anger management. And when you combine all those benefits, you're obviously just going to *feel* better. In other words, after ninety minutes of yoga—or even thirty—your body, your mind, *and* your spirit are more flexible. To this day, the post-yoga glow is the most satisfying feeling I have after any workout.

## YOU'RE NEVER TOO OLD TO BE FLEXIBLE

These days, yoga is an integral part of my routine. It's what enables all of the other exercise that I do—it's the foundation of my fitness, and it keeps me injury-free. I meet folks all the time who have the same attitude I did ten years ago. They don't want to spend time on stretching and flexibility because they think it's too boring—and they don't think it works. They believe that you're either "born flexible" or not. They think that stretching and yoga are too uncomfortable, and they don't see results fast enough. They don't want to put in the time because they think it cuts into their workout time, which is the complete opposite of the truth. In fact, pulled muscles (due to lack of flexibility) cause as many people to quit their fitness programs as joint injuries. Back and hamstring muscle strains and injuries can take as long to heal as broken bones . . . or longer.

Your body needs help to be flexible. That's where stretching, yoga, and Pilates come in. They provide all the textbook benefits you've read about a thousand times, such as reducing muscular soreness; increasing skill levels during training and athletic performance; reducing the risks of various injuries (like back problems, muscle strains, and joint sprains); slowing the aging process in muscles and joints; and improving posture.

Yoga, in particular, goes even deeper than physical flexibility. It improves overall body awareness by forcing you to focus on your breath and the sensations all over your body (unless you're checking out that attractive guy/girl sweating away next to you). When you're doing an asana—a yoga pose—your focus is on what your body is doing in the here and now.

Yoga also serves as a powerful detoxifier. Any exercise is going to help you detoxify—when you get your blood and breath moving, you draw in the $O_2$ and release the $CO_2$. But yoga is especially beneficial when it comes to aiding your lymphatic system. The primary function of the lymphatic system (a part of the circulatory system) is to transport lymph, a clear fluid containing white blood cells, throughout the body. Lymph helps rid the body of toxins, waste, and other unwanted materials. Yogic breathing and gentle poses are thought to help promote circulation of the body's lymph fluid. While all exercise will help your lymph eliminate this waste, yoga is specifically designed to flush it out more effectively. And who doesn't like a good flush now and then?

The main reason most people aren't more flexible is that they're unwilling to put in the time to gain flexibility. But I urge you to consider this time as an investment in your future—in your muscular health and functional fitness, in your athletic activities, and in your mobility as you age. Stretching and yoga are just as important as strength conditioning and cardiovascular fitness. They can help to restore the natural flexibility and durability we had in our youth. *Being flexible makes you younger.* Just think about it: In all the years you've known Gumby, has that animated rubber guy aged a day? Enough said.

Flexibility is the Fountain of Youth! Give yourself that amazing gift. Here's to touching your toes.

# YOUR BRAIN ON YOGA

Flexibility is just one of the benefits of a regular yoga practice. In Law 5, we talked about how exercise stimulates endorphins in your brain that help promote a feeling of well-being. Yoga is as good as any exercise at doing this, but where it really shines is how it releases a chemical called GABA (gamma-aminobutyric acid, if you want to get fancy about it), which acts as an inhibitor of neural activity, similar to the way many anti-anxiety drugs work. In other words, yoga mellows you out, dude. And more research is being published every day that shows how beneficial yoga can be for your mental and physical health. Recently, a study published in the *Journal of Sexual Medicine* showed that yoga can improve females' sexual arousal, satisfaction, and orgasm (ahem) by building their abdominal and pelvic muscles while improving their mood and joint function. And a study out of Sweden links a regular yoga practice with improved immunity.

## Four of My Favorite Stretches

You don't need to commit to a solid ninety-minute Hatha practice every time you want to loosen up a little. Look at dogs, cats, or any other species that intuitively know when to stretch. Every now and then, they love to get up from a nap and go right into up-dog and down-dog (even cats).

Whether you're a desk jockey, armchair quarterback, or frequent flier, taking the occasional break from sitting on your butt to limber up makes your world a better place.

Here are four stretches I find myself doing all the time.

**SURYA NAMASKARA A (SUN SALUTATION).** This is a quick, simple yoga sequence. Start standing with your feet together and your hands at your sides. Inhale as you reach your arms overhead, and then exhale as you fold forward with a flat back, bringing your fingertips toward the ground. Next, inhale as you look forward, then lift your body halfway up, so that your back is flat and parallel to the floor. Fall forward again, placing your palms on the ground. Step or gently jump back into plank position on the exhale. Now bend your elbows, lowering your body close to or on the ground. Press your hands into the floor, inhale, and lift your chest and shoulders off of the ground. Next, lower your torso, tuck your toes, and press your torso up so that your body resembles an upside-down V. Make sure you straighten your arms while trying to relax your shoulders, press your tailbone to the sky, and that your hands and feet are shoulder distance apart. After three to five deep inhales and exhales, look up between the hands, bend your knees, and step or jump your feet to your hands. Take one last deep inhale, then reverse swan-dive all the way up to standing on the exhale, and then bring your hands to prayer in front of you or down by your sides. Repeat for five or ten minutes or until you feel great, which you will.

I love this sequence when I'm really dragging or I've just had a great sleep. It wakes me up, gets my joints moving, and gets my brain functioning. I don't drink coffee, so it's like a caffeine substitute—only I'm using a source inside myself to stimulate my mind and body. You're using cleansing oxygen instead of caffeine for that get-up-and-go first thing in the morning.

**FORWARD HAMSTRING STRETCH.** Sit on the floor, both feet forward. Bend one leg, tucking one foot into your inner thigh so your legs resemble a big 4 and reach down to touch your toes on your opposite foot. The straighter you make your back, the more intense the stretch will be in your hamstring. Actively reach toward your toes while taking five breaths and repeat on the other side.

My right hamstring is seriously tight, so doing this stretch not only feels great, but also takes pressure off my lower back.

**SPINAL TWIST.** Lie flat on your back. Bring your right knee up to your chest. Stick your right arm out perpendicular to your body. Using your left hand, guide your right knee across your body toward the ground on your left side, until you feel a good stretch in your lower back. Look right to let your spine get the most out of the twist. Hold it for a few breaths. Repeat on the other side.

When my lower back is stiff, this fixes it after about five or six deep breaths. It's also good for detoxifying. So if you've eaten or drunk something you shouldn't have, a spinal twist can help wring out toxins from the organs.

**CAT-COW FLEX.** Get on all fours, knees under the hips and hands under the shoulders. Inhale as you arch your back like a cow, trying to find the ceiling with your eyes. Now exhale, rounding your back like a cat, looking down between your legs. Go back and forth between one and the other for five or six breaths.

I use this one to loosen up my neck, shoulders, and back, or just to make the people around me uncomfortable in meetings.

## FLEXIBILITY IN THE KITCHEN

I'm not talking about *that* kind of flexibility (there goes your mind into the gutter again!). The way you fuel your body and brain has just as much to do with your physical and emotional health as how you think and move—so it's worth mentioning how you can apply the Law of Flexibility to your diet.

As I've mentioned more than once, my eating habits in my younger years were less than perfect. In the sixties and seventies most of us didn't know any better. When I was a kid, we ate whatever was advertised on TV, which meant a constant stream of cookies, crackers, sugary cereals, Ding Dongs, Twinkies, cupcakes, pie, more cookies, and ice cream with sprinkles . . . if it was filled with junk, made of junk, or covered in junk, I loved it. You could have injected cream into a paper towel tube and I would have shoved it into my food-hole. A good lunch for me was a PB&J or Fluffernutter (Marshmallow Fluff and peanut butter) on white bread with Fritos, three pints of milk, and two ice cream sandwiches.

As a kid, I was addicted to fat, sugar, salt, and chemicals—and it showed. The quality of my daily food intake was so awful that I often suffered from depression, despondency, and fatigue. Typically by sixth-period math I was in a coma. I was logy, groggy, and foggy, and I had the grades to prove it.

By the time I got to college, I had moved on to hamburgers, hot dogs, and plenty of pepperoni pizza—three meals a day, seven days a week. In fact, I distinctly remember the electric hot dog cooker I had in my dorm room my freshman year. I'd stick four franks on eight prongs and basically electrocute the things, shove 'em on a bun, and that was my meal. Gourmet food! (Not.)

Even after my move to Southern California, the land of kale and quinoa, I continued to eat poorly. I didn't know better, I didn't care, and to be honest, I didn't think it really mattered. Sure, I was working out all the time, but exercise was an excuse to eat whatever I wanted. I was young and I got away with it.

At the same time, I was still under the notion that it was important to have the occasional cheat meal, so one day I decided to attack this massive double-bacon cheeseburger from my favorite local Mexican-American greasy spoon. It was a double-decker monster, so big that I could barely get my hands around it. I'd try to get through this same burger dozens of times before, but could never do it. I was about 90 percent of the way through it when I realized how awful I felt. This hunk of rotten, burned flesh covered in processed cheese and greasy bacon was making me sick.

So I got serious about my research. I began to read labels. I went to seminars and read books and hung out with people who knew better—nutritionists, other fitness enthusiasts, and healthy foodies who helped me realize that fast food, junk food, and other food porn weren't serving me. Soon kale, quinoa, avocado, arugula, broccoli, and brussels sprouts were replacing burgers and processed food.

After having a couple of bad experiences with chicken served at a local "health food" joint, I became a vegetarian/vegan, and stuck with it for about fifteen years. Then one morning I woke up and thought about how much I missed fish and non-nasty chicken and switched and decided to start incorporating high-quality protein into my diet.

And that's where I am today. I call it being a flexitarian. I do eat fish and chicken, but the vast majority of my diet is veggies, especially greens. I'll even go hog wild (no little piggies for me) on some elk or bison once in a while. I try to avoid caffeine, sugar and artificial sweeteners, gluten, alcohol, and too many saturated animal fats.

I used to eat salads twice a month; now I eat them twice a day. My point is this: Because I stayed flexible, I was able to find a way of eating that worked for me—mentally, physically, and emotionally. I didn't follow anyone else's diet dogma. Instead, I listened to the world's greatest nutrition advisors: my body and my newly educated brain. And as cues presented themselves, I took them.

I'm not going to tell you how to eat. The only person who can tell you that is *you*. When I returned to some animal protein, a lot of my vegan friends felt betrayed. But no one knows my body better than I do. I'm a huge supporter of the vegan lifestyle, but here's a little secret: I also stand behind my ovo-lacto vegetarian friends, paleo devotees, locavores, and Mediterranean diet followers. Basically, if you eat a healthy diet and it's giving you the results you want, I salute you. I'm the grand marshal in your nutritional parade. I proudly proclaim that you've found the Best Diet on Earth for you—for now.

Here's the trick. The "flex" in flexitarian stands for more than being adaptable with *your* food system. It's also about being flexible with other people and giving them a break when they find their Best Diet on Earth.

In other words, your way may be the right way for you, but that doesn't mean it's the right way for the person next to you. Your greatest intentions, if not well received, will ultimately turn to resentment. If you find that happening, if you're resentful of the way others eat—or they resent you—it's time to put the Law of Flexibility into action.

The law of flexibility isn't just about cultivating resilience in your own life. It's about adapting a perspective that allows you to take in information from other people without judgment, to respect and learn from different perspectives, and to be willing to bend your rules without breaking them.

## Knowing When to Listen to Your Body

When I say listen to your body, I'm not telling you to indulge late-night ice cream cravings. There is a definite set of dos and don'ts.

First off, it's important to know that we as a society have lost touch with the true function of food. Our brains are crammed with appetites and cravings that tell us to eat when we're not even hungry. For me, it's chocolate chip cookies. They're my kryptonite, and I simply can't have them around.

Second, today's junk food is addictive! In *The End of Overeating: Taking Control of the Insatiable American Appetite*, David Kessler, M.D., former commissioner of the Food and Drug Administration, describes the problem as "Conditioned Hypereating." He theorizes that packaged goods have been engineered to the perfect point of saltiness, fattiness, or sweetness. They just taste so good that you can't help but crave them.

So how do you listen to your body with all that nutritional static flying around? Believe me, it's doable. Here are a few of my strategies:

**DON'T SUCCUMB TO EATING JUNK.** If you crave it, it's not because you need it; it's because you've been conditioned to crave it, so . . .
**TRY TO SATIATE JUNK CRAVINGS WITH HEALTHY FOOD.** If a craving is genuine, you should be able to satisfy it with a nutritious alternative— because what your body is craving is energy and nutrients, not a whoopee pie. Try answering a sweet craving with whole fruits, or a crunchy craving with raw nuts or "healthy" trail mix.

**DON'T TRUST YOUR RUMBLING TUMMY.** Hunger is misleading. It doesn't mean you have to eat. It means you're used to having food at a certain time. A growling gut means your system is anticipating food, so it's started the digestive process in advance. Usually, if you can ignore these timed urges for a couple of weeks, your brain will teach your stomach to eat on a healthier schedule. Drink a glass of water instead. You control it!

**LOOK FOR OTHER SIGNS.** Your body has many other ways of telling you that you need to eat. If you can't make it through your workout, you're tired all the time, you can't concentrate, or you just feel lousy, there's a good chance you should increase your intake of healthy, whole food. When it comes to specific foods, brain fog or a lack of performance usually means you should eat more carbs (fruits, veggies, and whole grains). If you're having trouble recovering from workouts, you might need more protein (lean meats, legumes, whole grains, and raw nuts and seeds).

# THE THREE R's: RECHARGE, RECOVER, RELAX

*Sleep is the best meditation.*

—DALAI LAMA

There's a guy we all know. We've seen him at work, at our kids' Little League games, or he might even be a relative. Let's call him Joe B. Average. The "B" stands for "Below" and you're about to find out why. Joe was an all-star quarterback in high school. He had it all: plenty of friends, a beautiful cheerleader girlfriend, a bitchin' Camaro, everything. At his senior year homecoming game, a nasty tackle tore up his knee. (The lineman who hit him was huge!) Luckily, they patched him up enough to finish out the year. Because of his injury, he got a partial scholarship at a smaller university that had an okay football team. He started out with promise, but soon that knee became a problem. He'd never really let it heal properly, so it became an imbalanced mass of scar tissue. As things got worse, he didn't bother to fix it—

nor did his coaches. They cared more about the win/loss column than Joe's health. Recovery and repair would have meant time off the field. Soon his sports career was held together by ice, tape, and cortisone shots, until his senior year, when it all became too much to bear.

And just like that, no more football for Joe.

After college, Joe got married, took a sales job, and settled into life. Ten years later, he isn't living so much as existing. He hasn't exercised in years, insisting that any kind of physical activity makes his knee hurt. His thankless job requires that he stay into the evening filling out reports, so he gets home late and sleeps for five hours a night, max. To deal with his "on the go" work duties, he gobbles down any food that's convenient—a greasy sausage-and-cheese muffin at the drive-through in the morning, the catered office lunch tray complete with jumbo cookies and bags of chips in the afternoon. He drinks caffeinated energy drinks to stay awake, so on the rare occasion when he does manage to get to bed on time, he still can't fall asleep. Because he doesn't get enough sleep or exercise, his hormones are out of whack. He has trouble focusing sometimes and is pretty depressed. His poor choices led to divorce and a job he hates. He eats to cope with the situation, so he continues to put on weight. All of that extra weight puts even more pressure on his knee, which has also become arthritic. To top it all off, he's starting to experience lower back pain, so he's popping a few pain pills a day to take the edge off. Life seems to have gotten very far away from him, and instead of living his Big Picture, he's a miserable passenger on the journey.

If Joe was willing to take a step back and reconnect with his Purpose, do some soul-searching, Get Real, and hold himself accountable for the choices he's making, he might admit that exercising, eating better, and sleeping more would go a *long* way toward improving his mental and physical health. But there's something else that could help Joe immeasurably now—something that would also have saved him a lifetime of pain and frustration. Joe B. Average is in desperate need of the Three R's: Rest, Recover, and Relax.

Law 11 is closely connected to Law 9: Find a Balance. You need to balance your uptime with *quality* downtime. It's essential for healing, recharging, and maintaining a healthy mental outlook. Here's a breakdown of what I'm talking about:

**RECHARGE:** Recharging is sleeping and sleeping is healing. Recharging is vital if you want to be at your best.

**RECOVER:** Where would Wolverine be without his ability to heal? *Recover* means that when you're injured, you let yourself heal properly—that includes the microtrauma your muscles experience after a big workout. It means more than just sitting around until you feel better. Recovery includes supplementing properly, massages, foam rolling, and mineral baths, plus doing whatever recovery exercises or stretches you need, and visiting a specialist if your body isn't healing as it should.

**RELAX:** Snoopy and Bart Simpson are two of the most relaxed characters I know, and just look at their career longevity. *Relax* means taking steps to reduce stress, mentally, emotionally, and physically. If you really think about it, 99 percent of the stuff you freak out about on a daily basis doesn't matter (okay, 93 percent). As I often tell the stressed-out people in my life who feel like every second is a make-or-break moment, "Relax, man. Lower the stakes; it'll take the pressure off."

# RECHARGE

Back to Joe. Because he gets only five hours of sleep on a good night, a couple of hormones in his brain are causing serious problems. Lack of sleep stimulates the production of a hormone called ghrelin, which, as you may remember from chapter 7, tells the body when to eat. Not getting enough sleep also decreases the production of the hormone leptin, which lets us know when we're full so that we stop eating. In other words, because Joe doesn't get enough sleep, his brain's good decision-making power is hijacked, and he overeats and makes poor food choices.

Not only does being sleepy cause us to overeat crappy foods, but chronic sleep deprivation has also been linked to serious health conditions and the onset of disease. According to a recent Harvard study, sleep deprivation reduces insulin sensitivity—which inhibits your body's ability to properly process carbohydrates, increasing your risk profile for type 2 diabetes.

In a study conducted at the University of Colorado, researchers found that regular sleep deprivation has a powerful inflammatory effect. And another study published in the *Journal of the American Medical Association* suggests that a lack of sleep promotes calcium buildup in the heart, which, over the long term, can lead to heart disease.

Then there are all the benefits Joe would reap if he got a good night's sleep on a regular basis. His mind would be clearer and less foggy. Studies have shown that healthy sleep habits "reboot" your brain, making room for new knowledge. Simply stated, Joe would be smarter if he slept more. He would have more energy, make better food choices, and be less dependent on caffeine to get through the day. From a fitness perspective, if Joe slept more he'd have a better session at the gym. A study out of Stanford University found that athletes who slept ten hours a night showed a marked increase in athletic performance. If Joe simply got enough rest, he could recharge his batteries and be one step closer to solving a lot of his problems.

## WHAT'S ALL THE HOOPLA ABOUT INFLAMMATION?

It seems like everywhere you look, some expert is harping on the evils of inflammation, so I thought I'd take a second to explain it.

Inflammation is an important part of your body's healing process—like when you whack your elbow on something and have a goose egg on the point of impact a few minutes later. Inflammation is how the body attempts to heal you and protect you from harm. In the early stages of injury, that inflammatory response creates a little MASH unit around the problem, allowing white blood cells, enzymes, antibodies, and other "good guys" to fight infection and speed healing. Inflammation doesn't just apply to bumps and cuts; it also helps to repair the micro-tears we experience in our muscles from working out.

Acute inflammation from an injury is a good thing. Chronic inflammation is not. Why? Because chronic inflammation in the body is the precursor to several diseases and conditions, including some cancers, rheumatoid arthritis, atherosclerosis, and asthma. In addition, because pain is one of the protective mechanisms of inflammation, chronic inflammation means you're hurting all the time.

So, to sum up, a little inflammation is good. A lot of inflammation is bad—and we humans love things that amp up the inflammation, such as high-sugar diets, added stress, and a lack of sleep. So do yourself a favor and recharge, recover, and relax.

## THE DEFINITION OF SLEEP

The dog-eared copy of *Merriam-Webster's Collegiate Dictionary* that I keep on my desk defines sleep as "the natural periodic suspension of consciousness during which the powers of the body are restored." I, on the other hand, define sleep as the key to a successful fitness program, not to mention the key to a successful life. (I've emailed Merriam-Webster, suggesting they add this to their definition, so obviously it'll appear in the next edition. Look for it.)

While you're waiting, consider this: If you don't get enough sleep, your body will not receive the proper restoration it needs to succeed with any goal, whether it's physical, mental, or emotional. Sleep deprivation does not go hand in hand with achieving your Big Picture.

About 40 percent of adults experience sleepiness that interferes with daily activities. In the United States, roughly twenty-five thousand people fall asleep while driving *every single day*. If you don't have enough energy to drive your car, how will you have enough energy to work out, take care of your kids, be a functioning member of society? Of course, if you can't stay awake at the wheel, none of that will matter anyway.

## MY SLEEP SANCTUARY

My bedroom is a sanctuary. There's a big four-poster bed, bamboo sheets, plenty of down pillows, and a fireplace. I put a lot of time and effort into making that room perfect.

"Um," I hear the peanut gallery piping up again, "awkward. I don't need to know what your bedroom looks like, Tony." Relax. I have a point to make, and it's this: My commitment to bedroom awesomeness began in 1994, after the Northridge earthquake here in Southern California, when the television in front of my bed fell off a table and cracked in half. Up until then, I had a bedtime ritual that included staying up later than I should and watching David Letterman or *Nightline*, so I fully intended to replace my busted TV. Unfortunately, at the time I was very much broke—but as it turned out, my lack of funds was a blessing in disguise. More sleep and less TV was the smart choice, so I never replaced the tube.

Then I realized I didn't need a phone in my bedroom, either. I was usually too blurry-eyed to answer the phone in the middle of the night anyway, so I got rid of that, too. Then came the better bed, the bamboo sheets, and with every change, I slept better—and felt better. My recovery time, not to mention my workouts, improved, and that was an important and powerful shift.

Luckily, you don't need a natural disaster to learn this lesson. Take it from me: Your bedroom is your sanctuary, your cocoon. It's where you go to heal and recharge. If your cocoon is covered in thorns, it's not going to work. You need to make sure it's just right.

When you're training, you put all kinds of thought (and expense) into your gear: your skis, your bike, or your climbing gear. You also protect yourself from the environment. You hydrate. You buy the right footwear. You wear sunblock and a hat. These are things that we all do to make the outdoor training experience more enjoyable. Why would you not apply the same principle to rest? It's just as important to make the most of your Yin energy as your Yang energy.

## SOME SLEEP SOLUTIONS

The solution here is obvious. Get your sleep! There are all kinds of ways to make this happen. Here are a few that have worked for me (or for people I know).

- Take that sanctuary thing seriously. At the very least, get your TV and phone out of your bedroom. For that matter, get the tablet, laptop, and every other electronic gadget out of there, too.
- Kick the caffeine habit. Any drug that props you up is a problem drug. You might have some serious headaches for a week or two as you break the addiction, but it'll be worth it. If you can't stop it completely, at least stop drinking it by noon, or try swapping out coffee for herbal tea. Caffeine generally takes at least six hours to work its way through our system, though that can vary since we're all built a little differently. That 5 p.m. coffee run may still be keeping you up at 11 p.m.
- Make time to sleep. Turn off the computer in the early evening. If you're not tired yet, find a Yin activity, like reading, yoga, or meditation. For some workaholics, it may be uncomfortable to not pack every waking hour with activity, but in the long run, that recovery time for your brain will actually increase productivity.
- Set a regular bedtime. This is huge, and millions of Americans don't do it. Sundown might be a little extreme for most, but if you shoot for a time before 10 p.m., you'll still allow your body's natural circadian

rhythms—the twenty-four-hour cycle governing your physiological processes—to function properly.

- Try holistic sleep aids. I'm not talking about pharmaceuticals. I'm talking natural sleep aids like supplements and herbal teas. A lot of people have success with the hormone melatonin. Valerian root is also a great, albeit stinky, relaxer. Another option is a cozy cup of chamomile tea. (You probably don't identify me with "cozy," but I'm the guy with bamboo sheets, remember? When it comes to sleep, I'm all about cozy.)

I suggest that you shoot for seven to nine hours of sleep nightly, especially if you're training five to seven days a week. You might need less if you're some kind of genetic anomaly, but my bet is that you're fooling yourself. There are a few universal truths, things we all need: air, water, shelter, food—and sleep. Burn the candle at both ends and, eventually, you're going to get burned.

## RECOVER

Joe should have let that knee heal. It would have, quickly, but the gridiron called his name. He was young and fit and the human body doesn't like to be injured. We've become a society that respects the notion of "working through pain." Only problem is, we've taken it too far. If you're cranking out twelve biceps curls and your muscles feel like they're going to explode out of your arm around rep eleven, that's just feeling the burn and it's nothing to be afraid of. But if you're hurt—if something is bruised, torn, strained, or sprained—you need to let it heal.

Again, I'm going to ask you to learn from my experience on this one. I've had more than my share of pileups over the years, and the only reason I can still climb ropes like a caffeinated monkey and attempt to ski like a penguin with a jetpack is that when I do get injured, I take the time to heal.

## I'M NO STRANGER TO INJURY (I'M JUST STRANGE)

It was another amazing powder day in Blue River, British Columbia. I had already been skiing for four days, and on the fifth we were skiing in the trees, which is as good as it gets if you love powder skiing.

I had completely lost myself in the sheer joy of cutting and carving around these big, beautiful pine trees when—in a split second—I found myself wrapped around one of those green giants. One moment I was on the top edge of a tree well, and the next I was moaning and taking a mental inventory of all my body parts.

Inventory completed, I was pretty sure the left side of my rib cage had been reduced to splinters. One of the ski guides carefully extracted me from the tree well and my friends began to gather around. Luckily, there were five doctors skiing with me that day. One by one they took turns poking and prodding my rib cage. Amazingly, they couldn't hear any clicking or gurgling, and collectively they agreed that I hadn't broken any ribs. Phew!

After I returned home, the pain began to steadily increase, so I decided maybe it was time to get an X-ray. Lo and behold, the docs were right, no broken bones. So where was this pain coming from? At best guess, the doctor explained that I had most likely torn my intercostal muscles and slightly separated some ribs. That's why I had pain from my sternum to my lat. The prescription was simply ice, heat, and a little more time.

So guess what I did next? Did I hop the next plane back to Canada? Did I hit the gym for a celebratory core blast? Hell no. I recovered. I took it easy and let myself heal.

My run-in with that evergreen was not my first. In college, I shattered my knee on a stump when skiing in Vermont. In 2011, I tore my right biceps muscle during some fly push-ups on rings. This is what happens when you live outside of your comfort zone, so the risk of injury comes with the territory. Just like with my ribs, I put in the needed healing and rest time with those injuries. I saw doctors and worked with physical therapists.

My body's got some issues at fifty-five. Hamstring, hip, knee, and shoulder issues come and go. I do a lot of work on my own to deal with these issues through yoga, supplements, foam rolling, and a few other therapeutic tricks, but sometimes that's not enough. There's only so much you can't do for yourself. In those cases, I look to outside resources: massage therapy, active relief technique, acupuncture, and chiropractic when necessary.

But let me be clear: Taking time to recover doesn't mean you get to take an extended time-out. If anything, these injuries ended up accelerating the level of intensity in my training. The torn biceps forced me to figure out how to exercise for months without an arm. The bruised ribs forced me to protect my core during every workout. Both experiences made me fitter, stronger, and better in parts of my fitness that never would have improved if I hadn't been injured. When my biceps muscle was healing, I figured out at least twenty new ways to work my legs. There's always a way to get your blood and breath moving, even when you're recovering.

## REPAIR AND THE BIG PICTURE

Joe's knee also makes a nifty metaphor for the role of repair and recovery in the rest of your life. If something isn't working quite right and you don't take time to fix it, your annoying molehill becomes a debilitating mountain.

I'm not just talking about major traumas like the bank robbery in the previous chapter. Regardless of how minor an issue may seem, take the time to fix what's broken, even if that means a slight delay in your Plan. If you don't repair a roof when it first starts to leak, you can lose the whole house down the line. If you don't address that "one thing" that annoys you about your partner, it's going to spiral into an ugly breakup. If you don't repair any aspect of your life, you stand to derail your Big Picture plans completely.

### DIET AND EXERCISE: PROBLEM-SOLVING PANACEAS?

If you're already fitness-minded, you can skip this section because you probably know what I'm about to say. No matter what kind of recovery you require—whether it's physical, mental, or emotional—fitness and nutrition should be part of your plan.

Healthy food and regular exercise are a means to having the energy you need to find the solutions you're looking for in your life. If you're not exercising, you're not taking full advantage of the fact that exercise releases norepinephrine, serotonin, and brain-derived neurotrophic factor—feel-good hormones in your brain that are vital to, well, feeling good. You're also not giving yourself a break from stress.

Exercise takes mental focus and concentration, making it harder to dwell on all the other rubbish that clutters our brains.

Eating nutritious foods loaded with brain-and-body-boosting nutrients is also essential for recovery. Wild Alaskan salmon, raw nuts, and seeds are rich in omega-3 fatty acid, a powerful nutrient for boosting brainpower. Most berries contain anthocyanins, antioxidants that help keep your brain sharp. And the whole B complex is crucial to keeping your energy system working correctly. (As a general rule, whole foods tend to be loaded with B vitamins, so if you have a diet featuring mainly unprocessed foods, you're going to get plenty of B vitamins. Yet another reason to be a flexitarian!)

You heal yourself mentally and emotionally through food and fitness. Think of them as tools in your arsenal as you create the life that you want to live, as opposed to one you stress over, complain about, and slog through each day.

## ASK THE EXPERTS

### Dr. Roy Nissim

My body's got issues. Hamstring issues. Hip misalignment issues. Shoulder issues. Knee issues. I do a lot of work on my own to deal with these issues through yoga, supplements, foam rolling, and a few other therapeutic tricks, but no man is an island. There are just some things you can't do for yourself. In those cases, I look to outside resources such as chiropractor and active release technique (ART) provider Dr. Roy Nissim.

ART is a method of breaking down scar tissue to promote healing.

Dr. Nissim fixed my chronically tight hamstrings like no other. So who else would I go to for some words of wisdom about the Three R's?

**TONY:** What is ART, exactly?

**DR. ROY:** Active release technique—or ART—is a soft-tissue system based on an active massage technique that treats problems with muscles, tendons, ligaments, fascia, and nerves. Basically, you shorten the tissue, apply a contact tension, and lengthen the tissue or make it slide relative to the adjacent tissue. The theory behind ART is that various factors can cause your body to produce tough, dense scar tissue in the affected area. This scar tissue binds up and ties down tissues that need to move freely. As scar tissue builds up, muscles become shorter and weaker and tension on tendons causes tendinitis and entrapment of nerves. This can cause reduced range of motion, loss of strength, and pain. If a nerve is entrapped you may also feel tingling, numbness, and weakness.

**TONY:** So, for those of us who left our Ph.D.s in our other pants, ART breaks down scar tissue that's getting in the way of your body working correctly?

**DR. ROY:** That's about right.

**TONY:** How do ART and chiropractic jibe?

**DR. ROY:** Performing the soft-tissue breakdown prior to adjusting enables me to get to the joint more easily and makes the adjustment hold longer. In my opinion—because everyone has one—if you have a tight or overbearing muscle and you disregard the tissue and just adjust, the adjustment will not hold and the vertebrae will subluxate again. How I explain it to my patients is ART is the cake and the adjustment is the icing. Alone, each works, but they are most effective together.

**TONY:** What's your response to the criticisms of chiropractic? That it leaves your body in a vulnerable state?

**DR. ROY:** In the medical world, some doctors do not believe that we should be considered doctors and some still ignore us and prescribe their patients physical therapy. I feel that most people are not educated enough about chiropractic and don't understand the benefits it can provide. Some people say that once you get adjusted you have to keep going. The reason they say this is because once you get adjusted, your body feels great. You feel less tense and relaxed. This is because your body is not working as hard; the adjustment realigns the vertebrae, which takes pressure off the nerves and those nerves innervate all systems of the body.

**TONY:** But your personal goal is to get people so they don't have to come in every week or two for an adjustment.

**DR. ROY:** Correct. So I implement other things like strengthening and stretching. All of that helps people so that they don't have to come in. But I'll be honest with you, there are some people who want someone else to do the work. They ask, "Why do I have to do it when I can just pay you to do it for me?"

**TONY:** So obviously people who participate in the treatment and do the exercises get better faster.

**DR. ROY:** Correct.

# RELAX

Let's pay one last visit to poor Joe. As you know, he's stressed out. He says he can't work out. (I say he can.) He also continues to make poor food choices. He doesn't find pleasure in life, so he looks to junk food to fill the void. He relies on lethargy and convenience foods as time management tools for his "hectic" lifestyle. Externally, he's miserable. Internally, his system is loaded with cortisol, the stress hormone that can cause serious inflammation.

To sum it up, Joe needs to relax. Joe's life is going to happen whether he freaks out about it or not. What would happen if Joe took the unnecessary fretting out of every "stressful" situation in life? What if he saw a doctor and committed to doing the hard work of physical therapy to repair his knee, if he maybe started meditating once a week, if he consistently went to bed two hours earlier? The answer is that his life would be a whole lot more interesting, enjoyable—and relaxing, too.

Learning how to relax is an integral part of finding your balance. The Yang of life throws all kinds of stress at all of us. Your role is to recognize when it's time to get your Yin working and find ways to relax and restore your energy.

## Acute Relaxation

Another aspect of relaxing is knowing how to do it in a tough moment. Some people call this "grace under fire," but I call it "acute relaxation."

Life presents us with some major challenges. For the most part, when the cosmic pitcher throws you a curveball, the best course of action is to take a swing and then walk away having learned a lesson. You can panic and freak out all you want, but time will still pass and life will still happen, whether you stress out about it or not. We can't choose whether or not we'll be thrown the curveball—that's out of our control. But we can choose how we respond to it.

If you're thinking, "That sounds great, Tony, but I'm just not wired that way. I start getting anxious if I'm five minutes late to work, and my nerves and stress continue to build throughout the day," well then, you, my friend, are in need of some acute relaxation. Acute relaxation is the ability to calmly and rationally assess a troublesome situation as it unfolds—at that very instant when you want to scream, cry, or both. It's when you choose patience and curiosity over stress or defeat. Here's the math:

Problem + Patience + Curiosity = Solution

Patience means not freaking out or not reacting emotionally. Curiosity means asking the right questions to help find solutions. Have fear, worry, and anxiety ever solved a problem? No. Have they ever made a problem worse? Absolutely! They just divert energy you should use to be solution-minded. They're nothing more than emotional kerosene on your smoldering problem.

## FIVE STEPS TO SOLVING ANY PROBLEM

Again, I can hear the chorus chanting "Easy for You to Say, Tony" in the background. They're right; it is easy for me to say. It's also easy for me to do. And it will be easy for you to do, too. When you find yourself tangled up in a situation, here's an action plan for how you can relax acutely.

1. Stop what you're doing. Honestly, just STOP what you're doing.
2. Take a few deep breaths and try to clear your mind for a minute. Ooommmm . . .
3. Once you're calm, reassess the situation. Think about it objectively and rationally, not emotionally or personally. This isn't about you; it's an external problem that you need to solve.
4. Consider the solutions. Ask yourself not just how you can solve the issue in the moment, but how each solution will pan out in the long run, in terms of your Big Picture.
5. If you find a solution, great. If not, go back to step 1.

Keep in mind that some solutions take a little while to work. Not all problems get solved in a *Brady Bunch*–like thirty minutes (or twenty-two minutes if you don't count commercials). However, knowing that you're on the way to resolution is half the battle. Stressful situations are just reality in a pressure cooker—and if you got this far in this book, I think you have the right stuff to deal with *any* form of reality.

I don't consider myself Joe B. Average—and neither should you. So let's learn a powerful lesson from him: Get that stress in check. Exercise and eat right; recharge, recover, and relax; take on less responsibility if you have to. And get some sleep—at least seven to nine hours a night. Sleep, healing, and stress management are essential pieces of your Big Picture puzzle. Need to

Find Your Purpose? Take the time to sit quietly, rest, and reflect. Having trouble sticking to your Plan? Maybe you're burned out and you need a little R&R. Cranking Up the Intensity on your time spent in the gym, with the kids, or at work? Then you'll definitely need to schedule in some more recovery time. Working on Finding Your Balance? Don't forget to counter your Yin with some Yang.

## AND ON A FINAL NOTE . . .

There's one more reason you should recharge, recover, and relax: You deserve it. A little R&R&R is a great gift to give yourself. Maybe you've kicked butt at work and gotten a promotion by sticking to your Plan. Take a well-earned vacation to decompress for a bit. Maybe you've spent months being consistent with your diet and intense with your workouts—reward yourself with a massage or a nap. Heck, book a whole day at the spa!

The Big Picture is packed with opportunities to push yourself. And at this point, you have all the tools you need to do really big things. If you're on that path, if you're on your way to realizing your Purpose, then you're no Joe Below Average. You're Jay *Way Above* Average. And a guy (or gal) like that deserves a break every now and then.

### RELAXATION NUTRITION: SLOW AND EASY DOES IT

No, I'm not suggesting that you should relax your chewing to the point that the food falls out of your mouth (although that's not a bad idea if you're eating at Arby's). However, I do think there's a lot of value in the old saying "Slow and easy does it" when it comes to nutrition.

By slow, I mean *slow down when you eat*. Next time you sit down for a meal, take your time and enjoy it. It's not a means to an end; it's a meal! Chew each bite completely. Set down your fork between bites. Because you're giving the food time to travel to your stomach, you'll trigger your satiety with less food. Furthermore, there are enzymes in your saliva, so when you chew food well, you're not only making life easier for your stomach and intestines; you're also giving yourself a jump start on the digestive process.

And by easy, I'm not saying that you should grab a pack of corn nuts at the gas station for lunch. I'm suggesting that you *avoid getting caught up in the stress of nutritional math and fancy diets*. Don't get me wrong. I think science is fantastic. I love all the test tubes, Bunsen burners, and fancy calculations, but there is such a thing as too much of a good thing. Listen to common sense and listen to your own body. That's the simplest—and most effective—way to figure out the food math.

People always ask me for my preferred ratio of protein, fats, and carbs. I have no idea and I don't care. And this body that I've put so much work into, it doesn't care about those things, either. It doesn't care about exact calorie counts. It doesn't care about percentages. What it does care about is looking and feeling its best—and that just comes from healthy food and exercising every day. No math. No flow-charts. Some people love taking the complicated route, but I simply don't need it.

Of course, if you've spent a lifetime eating junk food, you might need a little educating—and that's when a nutrition plan can be helpful. But use it as a guide, not gospel. If you're supposed to eat a certain amount of carbs, protein, and fat, don't totally disregard it, but put more energy into focusing on the *quality* of those nutrients: lean proteins, fruits and veggies, raw seeds and nuts—these things are the key. It's hard to screw up when you're eating them. Life does not have to be so complicated if you are making smart choices. It's as simple as looking down at your plate and asking if your great-great-grandparents would recognize what you're eating. If the answer is yes, chances are you're on the right track. If the answer is no, you're no better than Joe.

# CONCLUSION

You know that old children's nursery rhyme, "Row, Row, Row Your Boat"?

*Row, row, row your boat,*
*Gently down the stream,*
*Merrily, merrily, merrily, merrily.*
*Life is but a dream.*

I'm guessing you've heard this ditty before. But have you ever really *listened* to it? Someone shared his interpretation of it with me years ago. I've forgotten who it was (I think it was pre–ginkgo biloba), but I've never forgotten what he said. It might seem silly to some folks, or obvious to others, but for me it really struck a chord.

*Row, row, row your boat*

Rowing signifies your thing, your work, your passion, your love, your plan. Your boat is your Purpose, your raison d'être (reason for being). So rowing your boat is all about the work you put into the plan that will fulfill your Purpose.

*Gently down the stream*

This is about showing up to do the work, but doing it right—consistently. Make like the tortoise and not like the hare. Don't hammer through life. Don't hurt yourself. Don't stress out. Don't freak out. Just make the call, write the email, attend the meeting, take the notes, do the exercise. Gently—not like the crazy person trying to row upstream. You can be intense and mellow at the same time. Then do it again the next day.

Moving "down the stream" means that you're moving in the right direction. You're paddling with the current and using it to help you achieve your goals. Find the flow and go with it. Violently kicking and punching your way upstream is no way to build a life. That's what Blockers do.

*Merrily, merrily, merrily, merrily*

If you love it, you'll look forward to doing it, and nothing can stop you. Your purpose brings happiness and joy to you and everyone around you. The sun is out, the birds are chirping. Hey, this downstream rowing is a blast!

*Life is but a dream.*

When you do all these things, when you row your boat consistently, productively, intensely, gently, and happily—life really can be a dream. It's a spectacular feeling and a wonderful way to live.

For the record, I don't feel this way about all nursery rhymes.

Humpty Dumpty sat on a wall. Humpty Dumpty had a great fall? What does that mean? Why are you sitting on a wall if you're an egg? And if you're an egg with arms and legs then you should be in a natural history museum. And horses can't fix eggs. Those hooves, are you kidding me? Plus it seems like a lot of effort for one egg. What happens if all the king's men and horses are working on the egg—and the French attack? That's just bad planning. Truth be told, I do remember where I heard this one. Thank you, Louis C.K.

## HOW I GOT TO WHERE I AM TODAY

I'm not a freak. I'm not a genetic anomaly. I haven't had my DNA spliced with DNA from a twenty-five-year-old Cirque du Soleil performer. And I'm definitely not like those rock stars who can torture their bodies with various forms of abuse and neglect for fifty years, and then still inexplicably kick butt for their farewell world tour. I'm a guy who got tired of being out of shape, miserable, stressed out, and broke. I saw my Big Picture, I put together a plan, and I acted on that plan.

Every once in a while, I remember how I felt back when I was young and scared of the world. Sometimes I'd get into a tricky situation, whether it was looking over my skis down a steep run I thought I couldn't handle or on a video shoot in front of a bunch of people with a thousand lights and cameras right in my face. Twenty years ago, in those moments, I'd feel what many people in those kinds of situations feel: panic, fear, and anxiety. It wasn't about success and joy; it was about barely surviving by the skin of my teeth.

By luck or by happenstance, I scraped through those situations. Each time, I picked up a little experience. Over time, that experience started to build. And from all that experience, the 11 Laws took shape. I created them as I've traveled through my journey in life in order to make the trip a little easier. These Laws became a sort of intuitive roller suitcase—one of those really good ones, with the wheels that pivot—a succinct, understandable formula that allowed me to go the places I wanted to go and do the things I wanted to do.

Anytime I've gotten stuck on my path (there have been a few times—and there will be more to come), I have looked at my life—and the lives of the people around me—for common themes in order to deduce some kind of greater pattern or lesson. Along the way I've noticed that people often want one thing but find themselves "stuck" with something else. Not only that, but even though they want something else, they continue making decisions that take them further and further away from that goal. Decisions that, deep down, they know aren't good for them. It's as if they're caught in some kind of decision-making riptide.

I, in particular, was an unhappy, self-conscious, out-of-shape, freaked-out, stressed-out, overwhelmed, clueless mess. (And that's a partial list.) Think of a negative aspect from anybody's life and I was there. Once I started to make a few good decisions and move myself in a better direction, I became addicted to change, whereas before, I was afraid of change. I wanted something better and it turned out I had the power to create it. Formulating some rules along the way helped me move forward on my path, move further and further away from the mime routines on the Santa Monica Pier.

And by the way, anytime I stray from the laws, I get in trouble, so I practice all 11 all the time. My workouts have a ton of variety and intensity. I rarely skip them, because I understand that consistency is the key to my physical, mental, and emotional well-being, not to mention my productivity and creativity. The way I eat, the way I work, the way I am in my relationships—I use the 11 Laws in all parts of my life. They've given me the willingness to take a pounding and come back for more without being discouraged.

Every now and then, I meet an older person who does nothing but kvetch and complain. I know that with every bitter mumble, his or her life is just getting smaller and darker. It should be the opposite. The older you get, the more you've done, so you're having more fun. If you do it right, you'll acquire an amazing tapestry of knowledge and experience. At that point, do you still have that much to prove? Follow these laws, and as you get older, not only will you get wiser, but you'll also get more (functionally) optimistic. Life will be about joy and purpose. Sure, there might still be hard work to do, but it'll be a pleasure if you plan it right. At fifty-five, I'm living proof because I'm looking forward to getting stronger and wiser with every passing day.

It's not hard to achieve amazing things when you do what you love. I do what I do because I love it. And I love sharing it with *you*!

## ALL THE RIGHT REASONS

Whatever you do, make sure you're doing it for the right reasons. There's nothing worse than the awful state of mind that's created when somebody does something to "improve" their life in a superficial way. Don't spend your life chasing happiness by trying to impress your friends, family, and coworkers. True happiness happens when your priorities are honest and authentic.

And remember to spend as much time on others as you do on yourself. It's good for others and it's good for you—more and more studies come out each year documenting how helping others is actually good for your health and a key factor in achieving personal happiness. That said, some people spend too much time helping those around them and forget to take care of themselves. Don't forget to take care of yourself, too. Find a balance. That's what the Big Picture is all about.

## I'M A LUCKY GUY

I'm a very lucky guy. I live a life I never thought I could have. I'm ten times more fit now than I was in my twenties. I'm out of the same old rut and doing things I never imagined—and I do them with confidence—most of the time.

There's no reason—not one—that you shouldn't have the same confidence I have, along with the same fitness and prosperity. There's no reason you can't take all that angst and fear you feel and flip it on its head, turning it into excitement and purpose.

I was driving to work at Beachbody one morning when it occurred to me how easy it all was. Because this has been my life for a while, sometimes I forget how it used to be. I take for granted how easy it is to just get up, work out, take care of business, do a little bit of laundry, answer some emails, set up the day, and then head off to work. Twenty-five years ago, just the thought of a morning like that would have stressed me out to the point where I would have stayed in bed or blown it all off to play with that damn Frisbee. But that day, driving down Pico Boulevard, I had a mental moment of clarity when I thought, "Boy, this is fun! Life is fun!" My life used to be a patchwork of misery, stress, and fear. Today it's a joy—and that's as a result of following the 11 Laws.

I've been teaching the laws for years on a fitness level, but this book is proof that they have much broader applications. Apply them to your job, your relationships (you married folks out there, be careful with the variety law), and your life. Yes, you still need to exercise and eat right. I'm not letting you off the hook there, but when the workout is done, when the salad has been eaten, look beyond that. What other parts of your life need revamping? Do what you love. Have a purpose and a plan. Attack them with intensity, consistency, and variety. Get real on reality. Stay balanced and flexible. Do your best and do it now. The future will sort itself out.

My hope is that the laws will help you the way they've helped me. Maybe you'll use them as is, right out of the box, or maybe you're like me and you need your own custom set. No problem. Feel free to use these laws as a jumping-off point for your own laws. (Don't do eleven, though. Come up with nine or sixteen. Be original, for Pete's sake.)

And by the way, it doesn't matter how fast your change happens. (It took me more than forty years, remember?) If it's going slowly, don't give up and hop to the next thing. Keep going. If the Law of Intensity is overwhelming you, focus on Loving It. Focus on things that make life awesome, active, and adventurous.

When your plan starts kicking into gear, you'll know. I call this moment "the Satori." "Satori" is the Japanese word for "awakening." I remember my Satori like it was yesterday. It wasn't one moment on a singular day; it took place over a two-month period, as my Power 90 program was picking up speed. I had finally figured out the right balance of diet and exercise for my body. I was getting enthusiastic feedback for my exercise techniques and ideas, even from critics. Total strangers were telling me that my program was helping them get healthy and happy. I could finally pay off my debts and not live hand to mouth anymore. Life was just . . . better.

For you, it might present in other ways. Maybe you'll notice that your moods are different, you have fewer dark days and more good ones. You move differently. You sit up straighter and walk with more pep in your step. You feel lighter, stronger, more flexible, more capable, less vulnerable, and more durable. You go from being somebody who doesn't want to do anything to somebody who wants to try everything. You're no longer trying to pretend you're someone else. You're not rowing anxiously, you're not rowing lazily—you're rowing merrily. You're exactly who you want to be. That is the best feeling in the world.

You want to have an awesome life. You want to do incredible things as you get older. You can and you will. These laws will help you do that because they'll force you to focus on being your best.

That's what I did. Now it's your turn.

# APPENDIXES

When I first sat down to write this book, there was so much Big Picture information I wanted to share with you that I could hardly stand it. It was a first-class challenge, figuring out how to organize it all. Luckily, I had the 11 Laws and, as it turns out, all the pieces seemed to fit together within those laws perfectly.

Almost.

As it turns out, there were a few very important things that just didn't quite fit, mostly because they worked across several of the laws. Supplements are an example. In our modern lives, it's only *realistic* that a smart supplement regimen will help you *do your best*. You need to have a supplement *plan*, that's for sure. Sups help dial up your *intensity* and allow you to stay *consistent*. You need to *balance* sups with real, whole foods.

So, to remedy this, I've added a few appendixes filled with miscellaneous information and musings. Am I stepping outside my own laws? Yes, but when you step back and look at the Big Picture, I think you'll agree that it's okay.

# APPENDIX 1

## TAKE YOUR SUPPLEMENTS!

When I travel, I have a separate suitcase for my supplements. I don't mean a big steamer trunk. It's a small suitcase I keep in my larger suitcase for my important pills, powders, and potions. It's crucial when I'm on a big travel binge, like a recent trip: five different planes, three different time zones, and more layover hours than I care to remember, all in five days. I rocked it like a hard-core highflier, but without my macro greens and miracle reds, multivitamins and minerals, I would have been dragging my behind.

Of course, there's more to travel survival than that. I keep my stress levels down, make sure I get enough sleep, exercise at every opportunity, and eat as well as I can. But those are all incredibly variable factors. The moment I lock my front door and roll my Briggs & Rilley down to my ride to the airport, I know I've relinquished control of my stress, sleep, exercise, and eating. One delayed flight and all that stuff can go topsy-turvy. Supplements, on the other hand, can remain consistent. They hold it all together for me. They're the glue in my plan.

# THRIVING, NOT SURVIVING.

"Stop the presses!" I can hear you saying. "Tony, if you eat like a king with a diet full of organic, free-range, homegrown farmer's market food, four or five meals a day, why do you still need to add supplements?"

The answer is simple. I shouldn't—and neither should you. That is, of course, provided you lived in a magical fairyland free of toxins and stress, where you can be 100 percent sure that the perfect meals you eat fit your exact needs. If your life fits all these criteria, then no supplementation for you! Enjoy your time on the other side of the rainbow, Dorothy. Back here in the real world—by that I mean here on dirty planet Earth—we need supplements to make the most of our lives.

Heather Fitzgerald is a registered dietician specializing in metabolic disorders, disordered eating, and successful aging. She's also the expert I look to for help with my supplement regimen. "My philosophy is that even if we eat healthy, most of our food sources aren't as rich in minerals and vitamins as they could be, especially if they're not organic," explains Heather. "Also, many women, in particular, don't eat enough calories to actually get all of the nutrients that they need from their food because they're often dieting. With all these factors in mind, we start to build an accumulation of deficiency. And supplements can help with that."

In our hectic modern world, we need a safety net to make sure we're getting the nutrition we need to survive, but that's not the primary reason I supplement, given that I'm not interested in surviving. I'm interested in *thriving*—as I'm sure you are. We try to push ourselves harder, jump higher, run faster. We make the most out of this amazing machine of muscle, organs, and bone we call our body. Why do professional athletes, gymnasts, football players, basketball players, and lacrosse players excel at such a high level? Is it purely because they eat three squares a day? Do you really think they got that way based on food alone? No way. If you want to perform, if you want to be athletic, if you want your muscles and your tendons and your ligaments to heal rapidly enough so that you can come back and do it day in and day out, then you're going to need supplementation to do it.

## AT MY AGE . . .

My reality is that I'm fifty-five as I write this book, but I'm not even close to winding down. I prefer to live large instead of loaf and lounge, so I push my body hard. If I didn't supplement, I'd have to deal with all kinds of issues, from lack of energy to joint pain, lethargy, and slow brain function.

At my age, most men experience a serious dip in hormone levels, most notably testosterone. (They're usually at about half the levels they were in their twenties.) When Heather gave me a blood test recently, she found that my free testosterone, the kind that's actually floating around the bloodstream, was slightly low, so she recommended 25 mg of DHEA daily. DHEA, or dehydroepiandrosterone (say that ten times fast), is a hormone made by the body that acts as a precursor of testosterone.

So, yes, even with all my hard work, I'm still feeling the effects of aging—but not as much as most. Here's the point: While aging is a reality, the high rate of decay that can come with it doesn't need to be. My testosterone was slightly low, but nowhere near the plummeting numbers seen in most middle-aged guys. Why? Because I take care of myself, and I supplement, that's why!

## AN OUNCE OF PREVENTION

Another great thing about supplements is that they're a form of preventive therapy. Instead of fixing a health problem, a good supplement regimen can stop it before it starts. "America is great at crisis medicine," Heather tells me. "We're number one in the world for emergency medicine but we're at the bottom on the scale for prevention. If something breaks or when you finally have that heart attack, we can save you, but we do nothing in order to prevent that."

You don't need to have an issue to benefit from starting a supplement regimen. Proper supplementing is a key component of functional—or holistic—medicine, which looks at the body as a whole instead of focusing on specific maladies as they happen. The reality is that everything in your body is interconnected, so if you keep systems running smoothly, you decrease the chance that something will go wrong. "It's all about prevention," says Heather. "Let's look at what's going on with you when you're in your thirties; look at your genetics, look at your lifestyle, what are the things we can change? That can make or break whether or not someone gets cancer. Cancer's all about cell breakdown, cell mutation, so protecting your cells through lifestyle and organic nutrients is key."

Obviously, that doesn't mean you should fire your physician. Following your doctor's orders is important. However, a proper diet—including a solid supplement regimen—can mean fewer visits to his or her office.

# SUPPLEMENTATION 101: FOUR SUPPLEMENTS THAT EVERYONE SHOULD CONSIDER

While working with an expert like Heather is the best way to make sure you're taking the right supplements, there are a few sups out there that everyone should consider. Here's a good list to get you started.

## Omega-3 Fatty Acids

"If I had to choose one supplement for every person that comes into the office, it would be fish oil," Heather insists. Your body is pretty good at converting dietary fat into whatever other kind of fat it needs, but there are a couple of kinds of fat that the body can't make itself, so you need to eat them. We call these "essential fatty acids" and there are two kinds: omega-6 fatty acids and omega-3 fatty acids. Both of these fats do all kinds of things in your body, such as regulating your immune system and your cardiovascular system. Omega-3s can also function as a powerful anti-inflammatory.

You can't throw a stick without hitting omega-6s in the American diet, so you probably don't need to worry about them. You'll find them in nuts, peanuts, corn, and most vegetable oils. Omega-3s, on the other hand, are tough to come by. "They're virtually absent in our diets," says Heather.

You'll find a little in seed oils—particularly flaxseed and chia seeds, making those things very important in any vegan's diet—but the most absorbable forms of omega-3s come from seafood. Here's where things get tricky. To get omega-3s at therapeutic levels, you'd need to eat pounds of fish every day. And even if that sounds like your idea of a good time, most fish also contain mercury, a heavy metal that can attack the nervous system. Don't worry, your body can process mercury in moderation just fine, but the four servings of fish a day it would take to get therapeutic levels of omega-3 fatty acids? Not so much. I'd leave the mass-quantity fish consumption to Shamu and try an omega-3 supplement instead. Specifically, seek out a fish oil omega-3 sup made from anchovies or krill, which are low in mercury. Also, look for omega-3 supplements that have been "molecularly distilled," meaning all those nasty heavy metals have been filtered out.

And here's another tip. Quality fish oil supplements give you "fish burps," but try storing the bottle in the freezer. I can't tell you why this works, but it does, so don't look a gift halibut in the mouth.

The benefits of this supplement are staggering. "It's used to treat body pain, any kind of osteoarthritis, depression and anxiety, mood disorders," says Heather, "I think it's probably the most popular and more accepted supplement in conventional medicine."

*Multivitamins*

I'm not advocating that you live like George Jetson and get all your nutrients from a pill. However, taking a daily multivitamin is a great safety net. Do you hit all your vitamin and mineral numbers every day? Even with that second helping of kale? What's that you say? You have no idea? Well, you're in good company because neither do I. But I know I increase my chances of hitting those numbers with a good multivitamin.

For the most part, too much is better than not enough when it comes to vitamins and minerals. True, you don't want to overdo a few of them, especially the fat-based ones, but provided your kidneys are in good shape, a good multi won't cause a problem. For the most part, you just pee out excess micronutrients.

Generally, you get what you pay for with supplements, so if you pick one from a reputable company that you trust and you avoid bargain-basement multivitamins, you'll have much more success finding a quality one.

Also, vitamin pills are held together by something called "binders." These binders vary depending on the brand. Certain binders can give some people stomachaches. If this happens to you, try taking them with food. If this doesn't work, don't give up on supplementation. Instead, try a different brand.

### Vitamin D

Vitamin D is a fat-soluble vitamin that helps you absorb calcium, which is crucial for maintaining bone density—something that becomes increasingly important as you grow older, especially for women. It also helps cells mature. (No one wants immature cells. They're not potty-trained and they're prone to temper tantrums.) Not a lot of foods contain vitamin D naturally—oysters, several fish, and eggs, to name a few. This shouldn't be an issue since our bodies can actually synthesize vitamin D, provided we have enough exposure to the sun. Back in the old days, when Pa worked the field all day while Ma chased the chickens around the yard, we all got plenty of vitamin D. But nowadays we all spend our time under artificial lights, leaving many of us in desperate need.

"It prevents colon, breast, and prostate cancer," states Heather. "There was a study that came out a few years ago that showed that patients who had suboptimal levels were more likely to have pancreatic or upper intestinal cancers. So, if you look at the country, you'll see in the Northeast, everybody's low in vitamin D and there is more incidence of cancers than there is in, say, Southern California."

So the solution is obvious. You all need to move out here to LA. I have a couple of guest rooms, so you can all crash at my pad until you find your own place.

Or, instead, you can get a good vitamin D supplement. Look for vitamin $D_3$, or cholecalciferol, which is the kind that your body synthesizes. Therefore it's the kind your body uses most efficiently—no sunblock required!

*Probiotics*

Aah! You've got bugs in your guts! Bugs, I tell you! Bugs!

Relax. So do I. So does everyone, in fact. The human intestines are home to millions of bacteria, or flora, some good and some bad, locked in a constant power struggle. The good bacteria help you digest certain foods; boost immunity; ward off cancer, allergies, and autoimmune diseases; and may even help you regulate your weight. On the other hand, the bad flora do the opposite and can lead to some nasty conditions like candida (yeast) overgrowth and leaky gut syndrome, where the lining of your gut is compromised, allowing pathogens to "leak" into your system. (I know! Heinous, huh?)

So it's important to send a constant supply of reinforcements to the battle down below in the form of prebiotics and probiotics. Prebiotics feed the good bacteria. You'll find them in beans and other veggies, brown rice, and oat bran. Probiotics, which actually contain strains of good bacteria, show up in fermented foods like yogurt, tempeh, and natto—a fermented soybean goo with the consistency of egg whites.

Supplemental probiotics are a great way to add good bugs and kill the bad ones. "It's always a good idea for anyone," Heather insists, "as a general immunity builder."

---

### Creatine: 1, Steroids: 0

I love steroids.

Now that I have your attention, let me clarify that a little. I think steroids are great *in some cases*. When used under a doctor's guidance, they have incredible properties that help people heal disease and shrink tumors. But if using them to look like the Hulk is your goal . . . well, let's just say that I know a lot of bodybuilders in their fifties and sixties who are on dialysis because they agreed with you. Get the picture? I just don't see the point of taking any supplement that, in the long term, does more damage than good.

Creatine, on the other hand, is one of the greatest supplements around for a guy my age who wants to do the things I need to do—or for almost anyone else looking to build a little muscle. There's a lot of stuff on the Interwebs about the negative effects of creatine and how it affects your kidneys, but that's pure conjecture. Even the Mayo Clinic recommends this supplement as a safe way to build muscle mass and increase strength. I've been using it for twenty years and my kidneys are still perfect.

If you're asking what creatine is, exactly, allow me to break it down with one of Professor Horton's Patented 100-Word Science Lessons™:

Creatine exists naturally in the body. We get it in our diets by eating meat. (That's another reason it benefits me, personally. I don't eat a lot of animal products.) When your workout is extra-challenging, you derive energy from special anaerobic (or "oxygen-poor") pathways. Creatine phosphate plays an important role in this process. By supplementing, you make sure you have all the creatine you need to hammer out that one last rep. Creatine itself doesn't make you bigger. It just makes sure you have a little more energy to push yourself a little harder.

Can you take too much creatine? Sure. You can also take too much vitamin E and vitamin D. That doesn't mean you should rule them out. If you have kidney issues, always check with your doctor first. Otherwise, it'll be obvious that you need to cut back your dosage because you'll either cramp or find yourself taking unexpected potty breaks.

I'm not saying we should start pumping creatine into the water supply. It's not for everyone, but it's a great option for those looking for an edge without using edgy supplements.

# APPENDIX 2

## FITNESS: THE HORTON TECHNIQUE

I've spent a lot of words in this book telling you that daily exercises should be fun and functional. Here's where I tell you how I do my part to make that happen.

Crazy eights, surfer spins, levers—to you these may be just exercises. To me they're more than that. They're the way I help you and millions of your closest friends turn your lives around. They're the primary way that I express myself creatively and that's why I love coming up with these moves. They're part of my contribution to the Big Picture. Susan Feniger makes delicious food. Jack White throws down killer licks. I create workouts that change your body and keep you coming back for more. I hope.

Almost every exercise I come up with is composed of two elements. They're multifunctional and fun. My movements and exercises are going to work several parts of your body—maybe different muscles, maybe different systems—and it's a fitness party, baby! As my P90X3 co-conspirator Stephanie Saunders puts it, "With Tony, it's never a push-up, it's a plyometric move into a sidearm balance into a core crunch—effective, functional, fun."

In a word, it's all about creativity. Adding creativity to exercise allows people to lose weight more rapidly because they're not focusing on training just body parts. They're focusing on learning the moves. Either that, or they're focusing on the aspect of the exercise they know they can do, but because it's a compound move, they're exposing their bodies to additional movements they didn't know they could do. They think more while improving their range of motion and balance.

The problem with most exercises is that they're linear in nature. Rowing machines and stationary bikes are great for your legs and arms because they raise your heart rate and get your heart and lungs to work, but they don't do much beyond that. A rowing machine helps you become a better rower and a stationary bike helps with your biking endurance, but I want more out of my valuable time.

My movements go beyond that. They require virtually no equipment, which is a nice thing, and they resemble how athletes move on a field or a court. Most athletes don't just move forward in a straight line. They're twisting, jumping, climbing, leaping, pivoting, spinning, or doing some combination thereof. This is how athletes move, whether you're on skis hurling down a mountain, executing a shoulder lock on an MMA mat, or scrambling across a soccer field.

Think about it in terms of a ball. I don't mean having a ball, I mean a literal ball covered with leather or rubber or whatever. Think of all the effort that goes into doing whatever you need to do to that ball. Baseball: hit the ball, catch the ball, chase after the ball. Football: throw the ball, run with the ball, catch the ball, spike the ball, and do a well-choreographed post-touchdown jig. Same with basketball, lacrosse, tennis, quidditch, or any other ball-based sport. We're no different from dogs, apparently, and that requires the body to go up, to go back, to go left and right in a quick, efficient fashion, typically while dodging a bunch of other players who also want that ball.

So all of my exercises are based on the idea of being able to do those moves better, whether you're playing team sports or scaling a mountain. For example, with my agility workout in P90X3, a lot of the moves start with an explosive movement, then go to isometric followed by another explosive movement, then another iso hold. Maybe you're leaping, jumping, and balancing on one foot, then you explode off that foot with all your energy and land on the other foot. You're working on your fast twitch, your slow twitch, balance, and explosive power all at once.

My Post Activation Potentiation (PAP) moves from P90X2 are another good example. You sequence a strength move, a plyometric explosive move, then an isometric one. The combination of those three things helps increase power, strength, and range of motion.

Every time I design an exercise, I look for an effective movement that's already out there. I think, okay, that's pretty good—how can I make it better? How can I make it more dynamic or increase the range of motion? Let's say I start with a standard walking lunge. What if I add plyometrics to the walking lunge? What if I add plyometrics and don't just go forward, but go backward, too? What if I go forward, backward, left, and right?

But wait! There's more! What if I went forward, backward, left, and right, and lifted a medicine ball over my head in an arcing motion?

So the backward motion increases work on the glutes, hamstrings, and quads. The sideways motion works all those same muscles, but in new and different ways. The plyometric component works on explosive power and, because it's a dynamic move, it's going to burn more calories. Then the medicine ball dials everything up to eleven by adding weight, which adds bonus work to your core and shoulders. You're working the entire kinetic chain in ways that you can't by just doing the simple first version.

In other words, you've gone from a boring old Phys Ed 101 snoozer move to something super-athletic. Athletes don't do lunges on a court or field! There's no such thing as an athletic lunging contest. So I do what I need to do to make the move really count.

Last but not least, I make sure that some moves are silly, to break up the intensity. A classic example is wacky jacks, inspired by Jack LaLanne's jumping jacks. I thought, "What if I do that, but pivot laterally at the waist at the same time?" Suddenly it became a goofy move that cracks people up every time we do it. But at the same time, it's a great way to work your intercostal muscles and obliques in a cardiovascular way. It also requires coordination. That's the trick to adding entertainment to fitness. I also need to make sure there's science behind all of my routines.

You don't need to worry about the science. I just want you to push, play, have fun, and learn to get better along the way.

# APPENDIX 3

## FOUR BIG NUTRITIONAL NO-NOs

Back in chapter 10, I discussed my flexitarian eating principles. If you're looking for optimal health, you need to let your diet bend and sway a little, not get caught up in the latest trendy diet dogma. It's important to choose your own path when it comes to food.

That said, there are a few ways that I'm *not* a flexitarian. Here are a few land mines I believe you're better off avoiding.

**REFINED FLOUR.** Whether grains are necessary in your diet is a subject of debate, but if you do eat grains, make them whole. This means the husk and bran are left on the grain, and that's where you find all the fiber and nutrients. Refined grains strip these two elements off, leaving just the endosperm, which is basically a nutrient-free blob of carbohydrates. If you want extra credit, eat sprouted grains, like you'll find in Ezekiel bread. They neutralize "antinutrients" such as phytic acid that many people, particularly paleo experts, feel make grains a poor food choice. Sprouting also increases the potency of the nutrients in the grains.

**REFINED SUGAR.** I have yet to meet a nutrition expert who likes refined sugar. Studies link the stuff to obesity, heart disease, and diabetes, and maybe even cancer. There are times when a little refined sugar can be used as targeted sports nutrition, such as after an intense workout to restore blood sugar and glycogen, but other than that, you should run, not walk, away from this poison.

**ADDITIVES AND PRESERVATIVES.** Start reading the ingredient lists on the back of snack foods. Acesulfame potassium? Sodium nitrate? Red 3? You know what that stuff is? (I do and, I'll tell you, it's more poison.) What would you do if, next Thanksgiving, your uncle Morty plopped a bowl of white powder on the table and said, "Here's a little butylated hydroxyanisole. Enjoy!" Would you eat it? I doubt it.

**"CONVENTIONAL" MEATS.** The reason these made this list has nothing to do with animal rights. The truth is, you are what you eat. Battery hens and standard feedlot cattle are fed a cocktail of hormones to increase their meatiness. They're also fed antibiotics to keep them healthy in dank, stressful conditions. Then you buy the meat, you barbecue it, you eat it, and—and guess who's consuming that cocktail now? No, thank you.

# APPENDIX 4

## SELECT READINGS FROM TONY HORTON'S LIBRARY

Read any good books lately? (Other than this one, of course.) If you're like me, I would hope you go through life as a perpetual student (only without the final exams and bad cafeteria food). Now that you've had a glimpse of the Big Picture, here's a list of reads to take your knowledge even further. These books have had a profound influence on me. I hope they do the same for you.

*Don't Sweat the Small Stuff—and It's All Small Stuff,* by Richard Carlson

This book holds a simple philosophy that helps you focus more on the important things and less on pointlessly freaking out.

*The Four Agreements: A Guide to Personal Freedom,* by Don Miguel Ruiz

Ancient wisdom from the Toltec Indians. It's a simple, easy guide to understanding how to lead your life in a less complicated way.

*Into Thin Air: A Personal Account of the Mt. Everest Disaster*, by Jon Krakauer and *Alive*, by Piers Paul Read

I read these page-turners cover to cover. I like books about real adversity because it gives me perspective and lights a fire under my butt to stop thinking about the silly stuff that slows me down. If these people can do this, I can take on my challenges, too.

*The Magic Lamp: Goal Setting for People Who Hate Setting Goals*, by Keith Ellis

Another book that helps you understand who you are and where you're supposed to be. Instead of being a cog in the machine or working for the Man, it allows you to find your Purpose.

*Man's Search for Meaning*, by Viktor Frankl

Frankl's account of how he survived the World War II Nazi death camps is inspirational and profound. Anyone who has ever struggled physically, emotionally, or mentally will benefit from reading this book.

*Meditation for Beginners* (audio book), by Jon Kabat-Zinn

A great resource that keeps the spiritual jargon to a minimum and gives you the basic game plan to start your own meditation practice.

*The Path to Tranquility: Daily Wisdom*, by His Holiness the Dalai Lama

A book all about the simplification of life. Daily quotes—

meditations on life—that you can refer to day after day after day, and year after year after year.

*The Power of Now: The Guide to Spiritual Enlightenment*, by Eckhart Tolle

Pretty self-explanatory, this one. It's a guide to understanding that the past is history, the future's a mystery, and all you have is right now, so make the best of it.

*The Road Less Traveled: A New Psychology of Love, Traditional Values, and Spiritual Growth*, by Scott M. Peck

I've read all Scott Peck's books. He's so good at giving concise life advice in a digestible way. This book features the foundation of his philosophy. It's a great place to start.

*The Seat of the Soul*, by Gary Zukav

The human spirit, our actions, and our words all have a connection to quantum physics. This book is another version of *The Big Picture*, in a way, but a much more scientific one. It's about how action, behavior, and thoughts affect the whole planet.

*Spark: The Revolutionary New Science of Exercise and the Brain*, by John J. Ratey, M.D.

Plain and simple, this book is about the science of exercise and the brain. You exercise and the brain is better. The brain is better and you're more creative and productive.

*A Thousand Paths to Tranquillity*, by David Baird

I bought this at a point in my life where, apparently, I needed more tranquillity. It's filled with quotes from the Buddha, T. S.

Eliot, Robert Frost, and others, all divided into categories like perception and honesty. It's just a great little book.

*The Tipping Point: How Little Things Can Make a Big Difference*, by Malcolm Gladwell

This book showed me, as a businessperson, how to understand trends. It helped me see what I needed to see to become successful.

*Touching the Void: The True Story of One Man's Miraculous Survival*, by Joe Simpson

Simpson is one of the premier rock-climbing authors. When I read about other people's sense of adventure, it forces me to be less timid and go have adventures of my own.

*The Way of the Peaceful Warrior: A Book That Changes Lives*, by Dan Millman

One of the first self-help books I ever read. It's ancient. (From the eighties!) It's about a young athlete who meets this wise old sage who helps him fight less and be more Zenlike.

*Younger Next Year: Live Strong, Fit, and Sexy—Until You're 80 and Beyond*, by Chris Crowley and Henry S. Lodge, M.D.

This is a simple book filled with simple rules designed to make the second half of your life better through diet, exercise, and lifestyle choices.

*You: The Owner's Manual*, by Michael F. Roizen, M.D., and Mehmet C. Oz, M.D.

An extensive source of information about what makes you tick. Required reading for anyone with a body.

# ACKNOWLEDGMENTS

The book you're holding right now wouldn't have been possible if it weren't for all the folks in my life who have contributed to my search for the Big Picture—but to thank them all would take more space than I have here, so let's just start with the people who helped me write what's on these pages.

First off, I'd like to thank Denis Faye, who waded with me through a bunch of scrambled ideas in my brain and then thoughtfully pieced them together with such brilliance and care. His patience made it possible for all my inspirations and revelations (even the 3 a.m. ones) to find their way into this book. He grasped *The Big Picture* from day one and gave it his all to make it come to life. *Merci*, Denis.

Then there's my unflappable editor at HarperCollins, Julie Will. Out of all the editors in this crazy, mixed-up publishing world, I feel I've found the true gem. She made it fun; she's super-supportive, and she let me write the book that I wanted to write. She really, truly understands the future of fitness and wellness, and her guidance was invaluable. Kudos, props, and thank you, Julie!

Special thanks go to Shawna Branon, who kept me on the straight and narrow, making things less about me and more about the Big Picture; Scott Fifer for sprinkling in just the right amount of humor; Bill Bondy and Bob Hennessy, who made sure my big-fish stories weren't too fishy; and Andrew Rice for his eagle eye and fine narrative guidance.

Of course, I wouldn't know what I know if it weren't for the experts I am lucky to have around me: CEO and mastermind Carl Daikeler, the lovely and talented Stephanie Saunders, Steve "The Human Guinea Pig" Edwards, Dr. Roy Nissim, Steve "Mr. Mechanics" Holmsen, Zen Master Ted McDonald, Heather Fitzgerald, and Jedi Master Ben Van de Bunt. These are people who have guided me, people I'm not afraid to approach for help and advice. Without them, I'd be adrift. Special thanks also to Siobhan Eustace, my first-rate assistant, who keeps me from wandering off into the woods in search of my van down by the river.

There are the folks who have honored me with their success stories, namely Richard Neal, Jeremy Yost, and Sterling Purdy. They've helped me understand the power of making decisions that can change your life. They're truly living the Big Picture.

And without the crack team at HarperCollins, this book would be nothing but a bunch of photocopied pages that I'd have to sell out of that aforementioned riverside van. Thank you so much to Karen Rinaldi, for running such a fine imprint at HarperWave, and Sydney Pierce, for your help with everything, not to mention Leah Wasielewski in marketing and Katherine Beitner in publicity. Cover designer Robin Bilardello and interior-design pro William Ruoto made the book easy to hold and easy to read, especially for old guys like me. And thank you, Harper Smith, for that cover photo. I didn't know I could look that good. (See what good lighting and makeup can do?)

Barbara Lowenstein is my nose-to-the-grindstone, tell-it-like-it-is agent. Thank you for all your hard work, Barbara!

Thank you to the Beachbody muse team: Jon Congdon, Jonathan Gelfand, Suzanne Blankenship, and Josh Horowitz.

The legal team: John Hendrickson and Nick Persky.

To my Monday-through-Sunday workout crew: Sean Callahan, Sergeant Joel Sydanmaa, Matt Sganga, Malachi Davis, Scott Fifer, Brendan Brazier, Greg Marusak, Phil Beron, Steve Glen, Alice Reitveld, Lauren Lobley, Rob Cowel, Jameson Hester, Travis Howard, Bobby Stephenson, Rami Ghandour, Anastasia Roark, Ashley Turner, Chuck Gaylod (and his boys, Alec, Ben, and Hank), Keith Queen, Andrew D'Amico, Brian Entman, and Donovan Tate.

Mountain maniacs: Steve Gartenstein, Dale Christianson, Paul Podell, Eileen Scanlon, Chris Snyder, Allyson Murphy, Stan Pennington, John Nicholich, Jim Walter, Tom Shuster, Rob and Kit DesLauriers, Jake Kilgrow.

Lifetime buds: Steve Eckholdt, Brian Donovan.

I'd also like to thank my family. Big Tone (aka Dad), who has been giving it his all since I can remember. And, of course, my dear mother, Jean, who continues to guide me along the way.

Then there's sister Kit Caldicott, the fittest, coolest Beachbody coach in America. Her husband, Danny, the fittest man in Massachusetts; and her kids, Matthew, Liza, Liam, who all live and breathe the Big Picture.

My other sister, Mary Beth Keefe, one, brave, courageous fighter; her husband, Larry "Tommy Moe" Keefe; and their sons, Andrew and Brian, two more young dudes looking to change the world.

Finally, I'd like to thank you. Every class I teach, every seminar I give, every copy of P90X I sign in an airport is an interaction—and I'm always listening to you. This book comes from you as much as it comes from me. And that's what *The Big Picture* is all about.

# ABOUT THE AUTHOR

Tony Horton is the creator of P90X, the bestselling fitness program in America. When he isn't developing a new workout, you'll find him in the gym or on the road, traveling the world to lead fitness classes for everyone from sports teams to members of Congress to members of the military. His training techniques have produced amazing results for celebrity clients all around the world, as well as professional and collegiate athletes.

Tony operates ASH Fitness, a private training facility in Southern California, where he helps his friends and everyday people meet their health and fitness goals. He is the author of two workout books—*Bring It!* and *Crush It!*—and he has recently launched his own healthy-food delivery service, Tony Horton Kitchen; and his own fitness apparel line, Tony Horton Fitness.

Visit Tony Horton at tonyhortonworld.com and on Twitter @Tony_Horton, his Facebook fan page, on Instagram, and on his Tony Horton Fitness YouTube channel.